PATH WAY TO PRES ENCE

a trek to intimacy with God

JESSE ALLEN

KINGDOM EQUIP

Pathway to Presence
A Trek to Intimacy with God
Copyright © 2023 by Jesse Allen

Unless otherwise noted, Scripture quotations taken from The Holy Bible, New International Version®, NIV®
    Copyright © 1973 1978 1984 2011 by Biblica , Inc.™
    Used by permission. All rights reserved worldwide.

Scripture quotations taken from The Holy Bible, English Standard Version®, ESV® Bible
    Copyright © 2012 by Crossway. All Rights Reserved.

Scripture quotations taken from the New King James Version®.
    Copyright © 1982 by Thomas Nelson. Used by permission. All Rights Reserved.

Editor: Deborah Raney
Cover Design: Jeremy Weldon
Formatter: Ken Raney

This journal belongs to:

_____

"What God in his Sovereignty may yet do on a world scale I do not claim to know. But what He will do for the plain man or woman who seeks His face, I believe I do know and can tell others. Let any man turn to God in earnest, let him begin to exercise himself unto godliness, let him seek to develop his powers of spiritual receptivity by trust and obedience and humility, and the results will exceed anything he may have hoped in his leaner and weaker days." – A.W. Tozer

Oil, Fire, and Wheat
*The oil of intimacy is necessary for our heart to carry a passon of fire
so that Jesus can inherit his reward in our life.*

Oil, fire and wheat are used as analogies throughout the Bible that uniquely articulate our journey with Jesus. Each of them beautifully depict the process toward God's intended plan for our life. Throughout the book you will see these icons placed undear each devotional. I believe that it is the oil of God's presence that ignites our hearts to live with a fiery passionate love for Jesus. It is this love that he wants the most, and is worthy to receive. Jesus wants to harvest our hearts as the inheritance of his life. As you read through this devotional ask God, "Lead me to intimacy with you, baptize me with passion for you, so that your Son can reap his reward in me."

Acknowledgements

I want to start by honoring four of my spiritual fathers, Rusty Allen, Matthew Penner, Samuel McVay, and Bob Pankratz. These four men have been crucial and critical in my journey toward discovering intimacy with God, identity in God, and walking out my destiny with God. The stories of this book, in large part, are all fruits of their investment in my life.

I am very grateful for my wife, who always empowers me to walk out this journey with Jesus with conviction and courage. This devotional couldn't have been written without her spiritual support.

Thank you to Tami Driggers who was instrumental in the writing of this devotional. From the idea for the book to the name of the book, her fingerprints are all over it. Without her encouragement and partnership, this devotional would not have been written.

Lastly, I want to honor and thank the Holy Spirit, the greatest teacher, mentor, and encourager a believer can have. My journey toward intimacy is not possible without his leadership. All I experience with God, and all I do for God is an overflow of my life with the Spirit of God. Ultimately, he is the author of my life and due the honor of everything that comes from my life.

Foreword

2020 was the year that altered the course of my life. I'm sure most people can relate to this statement. But for me, it wasn't the COVID pandemic that changed me, it was the Holy Spirit. In July of 2020, amidst the uproar that COVID was causing in the world, a small group of people dared to meet and invite the Holy Spirit to preside over their meetings. Co-led by Matthew Penner and Jesse Allen, the meetings were called "Kingdom Equip." Invited by a friend and completely unaware of what I was walking into, I found myself on a ten-day bender for all things Jesus.

Each of these ten days was marked with a hunger and intensity for the Lord like I had never seen or experienced in all my years of walking with Christ. While for some it may sound odd or even amazing, it scared me. A lot. All of my senses and logic told me to run. The worship is too intimate and weird. This is not real. Who are these people? And how are they speaking as if they can see into my thoughts?

The questions in my mind mounted with each step I took into the little church building where we met. More pressing than the questions though, was the deep longing and desire within my own heart to be a part of it. My soul was aching for an encounter with the living God, and I didn't even know it until I walked into Kingdom Equip. And encounter Him I did. Daily. Hourly. Every minute.

What Jesus did physically for the blind, deaf, and the tormented in the Bible, he did spiritually for me in those ten days. He opened my eyes to see him in a new way. He removed the blockage from my ears so I could hear him more clearly. He revealed the ways in which I was tormented and delivered me from the evil one. I had no idea I was held captive until I was set free. It was as if I had been living in black and white and now everything was in color.

As Jesse taught and gave testimony of his encounters with the Lord, I was captivated. This intimate relationship with the Lord he gave witness to, suddenly became something that felt within my grasp. As I began to believe this relationship was for me too, my whole world shifted. The veil that was over my eyes lifted and sweet freedom emerged.

—Tami Driggers

Introduction

Of all the tactics and schemes of Satan, one of his primary missions is to distort our view of the nature and character of God, keeping us distant from his presence and more satisfied with the pleasures of the world than with him. For so long, I lived under the umbrella of a false narrative of who God is. I understood him as a being of might and power, easily disturbed, quickly angered, and honestly, quite annoyed by me. While no one ever taught me this, it was the unspoken understanding of my heart. It led me to a Christian life of striving that left me feeling unworthy, unwanted, and purposeless. When I looked in the mirror, I saw an incapable failure who would never measure up. Ultimately, this all left me dissatisfied with God and disappointed in myself.

What I realized was that I had been duped. The character and nature of God that I thought I firmly understood began to break down. I began to see God for who he really is, a close Father who is full of compassion, mercy, and tender love. I realized that the God I was reaching for had already been reaching for me. Before, I was bewildered by God; now, suddenly, as I genuinely beheld him, I saw his beauty. I saw a man of hunger, desire, and passion. I saw a lover's beauty rather than a king's wrath. My heart now exploded with fascination rather than fear.

The journey of intimate knowledge began. The pathway to his presence suddenly appeared. I started learning what I didn't know, realizing I had to unlearn what I did. I imagine many can find themselves in a similar boat. One where effort, discipline, and striving steer the ship. I believe Jesus is walking on the water beside these boats with a hand extended, saying, "Follow me, I want to be in your presence; and trust me, you definitely want to be in mine." It will take trust and dependence to step out of what we do know, if we are going to step into what we don't.

I want to emphasize that this devotional is my personal experience with God, not added revelation to God. It is in vulnerability that I share my story with you, knowing that it may be misunderstood and scrutinized. However, I want to preface my story by stating that my subjective experience with God is always measured with the objective word of God (the Bible). My experience is not the precedent for a Christian life. My hope is that as you read through this devotional you will be provoked to hunger and thirst for God, diving deep into his written word and then begin to have your own encounters with the living Word, Christ Jesus.

During the next forty days, Jesus is inviting you on a journey to embrace his presence and encounter his love. He wants to write a new narrative on the tablet of your heart, dismantling the depictions you have of him that are faulty and depositing ones that are true and sure. He is extending an invitation, whispering with love, "Take me by the hand, and let me lead you to the promised land."

A Word about Journaling with God

My heart is for you to be propelled into the presence of God, having your own encounters with his glory. Perhaps, as you read my testimonies, the Lord will provoke you with hunger and touch you with his love. I have found that one of the best ways we can converse with Jesus is by asking him questions. At the end of each devotion, I have posed a question for you to meditate on with the Lord. As you do, ask him more questions, make bold requests, and write him passionate love letters.

TABLE OF CONTENTS

Section 1	21
Section 2	39
Section 3	72
Section 4	107

SECTION 1
Pathway through Passion

God's passion is what fuels our breakthroughs and brings about our victories. God wants to take his passion and impart it into our heart. With the same zealous jealousy that he has for his Son, he wants to be an all consuming fire of love in our life. The path that is being paved into his presence is marked with his passion. Walking this path will result in and require passion in our hearts.

Seal of Fire

God's jealousy is the fuel for our soul being filled and our heart being sealed with the fire of his love.

My life dramatically changed in the fall of 2016. I had been at a discipleship training school for roughly a month and a half. Each week we had approximately thirty hours of phenomenal teaching from various people. The teachings were profound and revelatory, opening my eyes to the Kingdom of God and the nature of Jesus Christ.

However, there is one particular morning I will never forget. All week Randy, a guest speaker, had been teaching on the authority that we have been given in Christ. He taught upwards of twenty-five hours that week, blowing my mind as he opened up the Word of God in a fresh, new way.

He walked into class Friday morning, intently looked around the room, and said, "There is no person on planet earth who is my best friend. My wife is not my best friend. The Holy Spirit is my best friend." At that moment, my spiritual jaw dropped wide open. At the time, I would not have been able to articulate it this way, but it was as if oil from heaven was being released from Randy's mouth. My heart turned, and inwardly I shouted, "If that is real, I have to have it."

Randy had told us how he got up at five AM every morning with his cup of coffee to commune with the Spirit. I had no context to even dream of waking up that early to be with God. But I thought, if it works for Randy, I wonder if it will work for me. The next day I woke up bright and early, put on a pot of coffee, and ran up to the prayer room that was located on the highest floor of the apartment complex we were staying in. I was hungry, desperate, and deeply desiring an encounter with God.

I am not sure why, but that first morning I was in the prayer room, I got down on my knees, placed my Bible beside me, and told God, "I am not opening my Bible until you meet me the way you met Randy." You see, at that time, the Bible was as boring as boring gets for me. It made no sense, and when I tried to read it for more than five minutes, I began to fall asleep. I heard my whole life it was "active, living, breathing, and alive." But to be honest, I found it boring, somewhat pointless, and irrelevant to my life.

Day after day, I went up to that room, singing praises to the Lord, persistently asking him to encounter me the way he encountered Randy. Three days passed. Then five. Then seven. All of the sudden, on day fourteen, I was once again on my knees praying to God when what felt like fire rushed through my whole body. Up to this point, I had never experienced something like this in my life. I simply sat there for minutes as what felt like hours continued. God was near. He was nearer than my skin and more real than what I could see.

While there are countless testimonies of the reality of that encounter, the greatest one I can give is the hunger and desire I instantly had for his Word. I opened up the Bible, and what once felt boring came alive. What once put me to sleep began to keep me up at night. The best way I know how to describe what the Bible became for me comes from the words of Jesus, "Man shall not live on bread alone, but every word that comes from the mouth of God." Matthew 4:4 (NIV) Suddenly, the Word of God gave more satisfaction to my soul than food did to my stomach. I became overwhelmed by his love and obsessed with his words.

He pursued me, provoked me, and then placed his seal of fire upon me. Everything changed. Since that day, I have been on a journey of learning about his love. He continued to teach me what I didn't know while asking me to let go of a lot I did know.

I was blinded to what was available to me in Christ. I didn't know what I didn't know. I wasn't aware his love was so fierce, passionate, and near. I thought it was an aspect of God that existed far off in heaven. I didn't know it was experientially available to me now. He peeled back the blinders and let me see, feel, and touch his love. It changed my life.

To be honest, I do not remember anything else Randy said during the remainder of his teaching that week. I also doubt the phrase that helped shift the trajectory of my life meant anything to anyone else. But to me, it meant everything. This is a point that should be stated loud and clear. One word from a mouth partnering with the heart of God can shift the trajectory of another's life forever. Randy's did to me. Yours can to others.

Like me, God is wooing each of us to himself. He is pursuing you with passion, wanting to provoke you to himself through others' testimonies, so he can set his seal of fire upon your heart. Today, lean in with passion and let go of the boxes you have put him in; he wants to lavish you with his love.

Is the Holy Spirit your best friend?

Consider what makes someone a best friend and what it would mean for the Holy Spirit to carry this title in your life.

Date: _____

Coffee with God

"There is not in the world a kind of life more sweet and delightful, than that of a continual conversation with God; those only can comprehend it who practice and experience it."
—Brother Lawrence

Growing up, I didn't know the voice of God. I didn't know it was possible to hear him. Of course, I knew that he spoke through the Bible and that its words were from him. But hearing his voice as I hear yours? I didn't know that was possible. If I had heard others say they did, I would have labeled them crazy.

That all changed one evening nearly six years ago. The week after my encounter with God in the upper room of the apartment complex we were staying in, we participated in a two-day "silent retreat." The time was designed to listen and talk with God. Coming in, we were challenged to express what expectations we had for the next two days. Right away, I shared that I would love to experience God like never before. Next, they said to surrender those expectations. So I did. To be honest, I never thought much of that expectation again.

It is ten PM on the first night of the silent retreat, and I am sitting outside on a lawn chair when I unexpectedly feel God lean in and ask if he can join me. Not sure if I am hearing God or if I am simply making up thoughts in my mind, I continue to sit there silently. Not a minute later, my heart begins to pound, and like a rushing wind, the voice floods my heart again, "Can I join you?"

I responded with excitement, "Of course!" Then a small whisper inside of me responded, "Pull me up a chair." I felt a little strange, but slowly I grabbed another lawn chair and set it down across from me. I am sitting in my chair drinking my coffee, thinking, "Is God really here with me? Honestly, I believe he hears when I speak, but is he speaking to me? Is he here with me?"

Unexpectedly, a voice rose in my heart as God asked, "Can you get me a cup of coffee?" I sat there for a few minutes thinking, "There is no way God really wants me to go get him coffee." Then I heard that still small whisper again say, "Of course I do." At this point, I was all in. I ran to the living area and refilled my cup, then grabbed another cup and filled it to the brim.

Remember, we were on a silent retreat so we couldn't talk to any other participants about what I am experiencing. The room where I got the coffee was filled with people silently sitting, watching me grab two cups of coffee at nearly eleven o'clock at night. I notice the strange looks as I imagine what they might be thinking, "Why do you have two cups of coffee? Don't you know what time it is?" I so badly wanted to tell them that God and I are having coffee together! But, I restrained myself and ran back outside.

I placed the coffee on the chair across from me. For the first time in my life, I felt like I had just "hung out" with God. It was me and him having coffee, shooting the breeze, and talking about life. I heard no audible voice and saw no face, but that night, I talked, listened, laughed, and cried while having coffee with God.

When I first expressed to the group that I would love to experience God in a way like never before, I hoped to hear an audible voice, have a clear dream, or maybe a vivid vision. Upon reflecting on the experience I did have, I found that what I had asked for became a reality. I encountered God "in a way like never before." God revealed himself to me in a way I couldn't have imagined. His voice led me to an encounter. Into intimacy. Into relationship. I found that God's deepest longing isn't for us to look up and speak to Him. His deepest longing is to invite us to come and sit across from him, so he can listen and talk with us.

This encounter started a lifestyle of friendship with God. I thought his voice was stagnant and could only be heard as I opened the Bible. I didn't know God wanted to sit across the table from me, commune with me, and talk to me. He began to teach me that his love is the fruit I get to receive from friendship, not the reward that I have to earn in duty.

I promise you, as he did with me, God wants to encounter your heart. He wants you to hear his voice. He wants to lead you into intimacy and a relationship like you have never had before. Simply listen, respond, and embrace; he's not far away.

> "The sheep recognize the voice of the true Shepherd, for he calls his own by name
> and leads them out, for they belong to him. And when he has brought out all his
> sheep, he walks ahead of them and they will follow him,
> for they are familiar with his voice."
> —John 10:3-4 (NIV)

How does God want to speak with me today?

Are you willing to engage your imagination with the Lord? Our imagination is part of engaging God with childlike wonder. Giving God access to your mind in this way will open up a whole new pathway to his presence in your life. Today, pull up a chair and imagine having coffee with Jesus. As you do, ask him questions and let him speak to you. Spend some time journaling about your time with God.

Date:

A Royal Diadem

"We are the reward of the lamb's suffering." —The Moravians

Of all God has, how can he want? How can a God who created everything want anything? He wants because he loves. He wants because what he desires most wanders away from him. Though God has complete reign and authority over both heaven and earth, he still yearns with a longing for you and me. Though he knows yesterday, today, and tomorrow belong fully to him, he jealously longs to attain something that is not yet his. This isn't just our subjection to his leadership; more so, it is our free will love for his Son.

I say all this to emphasize the fact that of all God has and all that he wants to get, you and I are the treasure he deeply longs for. I wonder, do you view people the way God does? Do you consider them precious like Christ does? I will go first. No. So often, I find myself busy doing things for the Lord while neglecting what he loves and values the most, people. I pass up opportunities left and right because, if I'm being honest, I do not value what God values.

I say this with vulnerability and conviction. I am now in a pursuit to understand the heart of God. To learn what he wants. What he loves. What he desires. If I am not intentional, I know what I will do. I will get what I want, all the while, believing I am investing in the Kingdom of God, but missing what he values the most.

This simple truth became a profound epiphany for me one day. As I was praying from Ephesians Chapter 1, I immediately jumped to verses 17-20, as I often do. As I read verse nineteen, I was awestruck. Paul prayed, "I keep asking that the God of our Lord Jesus Christ, the glorious Father, may give you the Spirit of wisdom and revelation, so that you may know…the riches of his glorious inheritance in his holy people."

I sat back in my chair and gasped. Jesus's reward is us. His glorious inheritance is me. It's you. Again, I knew this in my mind. But what I knew in my head was void of revelation in my heart. Suddenly, what I thought I knew, I actually began to know. I, we, are the reward of Jesus's suffering. We are the royal diadem in the hand of God the Father that is being presented to God the Son. We are the crown of splendor. We are the apple of his eye. (Is. 62:3; Deut. 32:10.)

Suddenly, I realized. I am attempting to store up treasures in heaven, doing things for God without serving the heart of God. The heart of God literally beats to give his Son what he wants the most. Us. Immediately I fell to my knees and began to cry out to God, "Make my heart beat to give Jesus what he wants most in me. Make my heart beat with a mission for people. Strip off the busyness of my life that makes me feel productive for you because it empowers me to neglect what is precious to you."

My guess is that many of us can relate to neglecting to care for others. Tasks become paramount in our ministry when our hearts aren't fellowshipping with God's. I found this to be true. I still do. But suddenly, as I embraced the heart of God, seeing what was most valuable to the Son of God, I became much more flexible with my time. Much more present. Much more empathetic. Much more interested in others' hearts than my to-do lists. Though I'm not perfect at it, this simple revelation has had one of the most profound impacts on my daily life with God.

This leads me to state an utter truth: We do not get back yesterday, and we are not guaranteed tomorrow. What we have is now. What is of highest value is people. Don't neglect people because you are too busy running errands, preoccupied with your to-do lists, or too focused on pleasing yourself and doing what you love. Who you have in your life today may not be in your life tomorrow. Who you bump into at Walmart and the opportunities you have to engage your waitress at the restaurant may never come again. Engage people with intentionality. Engage them from the perspective of God. Share with them the love of God. Give your life to serve people, and I promise you, you will never regret yesterday or be left unfulfilled today.

> *"You will be a crown of splendor in the Lord's hand,*
> *a royal diadem in the hand of your God."*
> —Isaiah 62:3 (NIV)

Is my heart in sync with God's?

Do you feel about people the way God does? Are you willing today to let go of your busyness that keeps you preoccupied from embracing relationships with people? Who today does God want you to engage with intentionality? To reach out to in love? To listen to with compassion? And to encourage with hope? Ask the Lord to bring to mind a specific person he wants you to bless, and then write them a note, give them a call, or sit down and have coffee with them.

Date: _____

A Culture of Honor

"A culture of honor is celebrating who a person is without stumbling over who they are not." —Bill Johnson

As I have continued to lean into the lives of people with greater intentionality, considering them royal diadems in the hand of God, I quickly learned there was a piece of the culture of the Kingdom of God I didn't carry.

One day, while I was reading Matthew 6:33, "Seek first His Kingdom and His righteousness," the Lord stopped me in my tracks, asking, "Do you know the culture of the Kingdom of God?" I sat back in my chair and thought to myself, "What is heaven like?" I didn't have an answer. But a longing for discovery was imparted into my heart at that moment, and I said to God, "I want to know!" He replied, "Strap in; let's go!"

As I dialogued with the Lord, I asked him, "What is the Kingdom of God?" He replied, "It is the reign and rule of my leadership. Every reality in heaven is merely a manifestation of my reign." I then asked, "How does heaven touch earth?" He replied, "Simple, the heart of humanity submitting to the reign of my leadership." He continued by asking, "Jesse, do I reign on the throne of your heart, or do you?" I was stuck as I wanted to say, and even thought, "You do, Jesus!" As the words came out of my mouth, Jesus responded without hesitation, "Would you let me examine your heart?" I thought to myself, why not? So I responded, "Sure, Lord, go ahead."

As he did, the result of the examination was unexpected. I sat there in my chair as Jesus said to me, "Can I show you the results?" I responded with emphatic excitement, "For sure, Lord!" Suddenly I started to feel bitterness and criticalness toward some of those closest to me. It was a feeling that was out of left field. I thought, "Why am I feeling all these negative emotions right now?" The Lord responded, "Those are the test results." He continued by saying, "Where I reign, honor resides. My culture is one of honor, not criticism." Jesus said, "Jesse, you reign on the throne of your heart, not me. And the evidence is found in what you just felt."

My heart was grieved as I realized the culture of my life was one that called people out for what they were not rather than calling them up into who they were created to be. I saw them through the lens of their brokenness. But Jesus said to me, "I see them through the lens of their destiny. I don't see them as they are; I see them as they were created to be. I don't call them out for their faults; I fight for the gold that is in their hearts." He then responded, "Would you?"

I cried to God and said, "Yes! What do I need to do?" He responded gently, saying, "This will be a journey, Jesse. You are a self-centered Christian who wants the glory that is due me. You reign on the throne of your heart. Your preferences and opinions are paramount in your life. You judge everyone who thinks differently than you and compete against those who threaten you. You need to be healed, my son."

These words cut like a sword, but I knew they were true. I felt the weight of how my heart of criticism had violated so many of my friends and family. How I compete in anger with those God gave me as gifts. As a result, I began to see how my words were weapons of destruction, tearing down those I claimed to love. More so, proclaiming words of love for God but dishonoring those made in his image.

I asked God, "How do I change?" He said, "The breaking of this culture doesn't come in one moment. It is a lifestyle you have to choose to live daily. Over time, I will change you if you willingly embrace my heart." I have been on this journey ever since. The journey of humbly recognizing how prone I am to cultivate a culture within my own life that is in direct conflict with the culture of the Kingdom of God. Recognizing the personal hypocrisy that dwells within my heart, saying, "God, I love you," and then turning around and spitting on his creation.

I wish I could tell you I am healed. That I am a man who honors every person who is placed in my path and constantly calls people up into their destiny rather than calling them out for their faults. But, nearly four years after the above encounter, I am still on a journey of submission to the leadership of Jesus. I am on a journey of honor. One of seeing people from the lens of the Father and interacting with them from the heart of God. I am on a journey of allowing my tongue to be a vessel of blessing rather than a sword of destruction, my heart to be a house of celebration rather than a home for condemnation, and my mind to be a magnet for the majestic thoughts of God rather than the destructive criticisms of Satan.

I imagine the testimony I give likely resonates with others, as the natural human heart is prone to a culture of criticism rather than honor, and our mouths are prone to cursing rather than blessing. But like me, Jesus is inviting you to embrace his heart and see from his perspective those whom you are most prone to see as problematic. If you will embrace this journey of turning from criticism to honor, you will start to prophesy his heart, fighting for the gold within the hearts of everyone you encounter rather than being a fault-finder who publishes the mishaps of all those around you.

Today is the day to start hosting a house of honor within your heart. To submit to the reign of Christ and seek first the realities of the Kingdom of Heaven. I promise if you do, everything else you need for transformation will be added unto you!

> *"So from now on we regard no one from a worldly point of view. Though we once regarded Christ in this way, we do so no longer."*
> —2 Corinthians 5:16 (NIV)

Who can I honor that I often criticize?

Invite the Lord to bring to mind anyone you may have criticized in word or thought. Repent of agreeing with a critical spirit, and ask God to replace your criticism of them with honor for them. Ask the Lord, how he sees this person and what his heart is for them? Write down what you hear God say and spend some time praying for them. If you don't feel the criticism lift, continue to persist in blessing them until it does.

Date: _____

The Real Thing

"I'm losing my religion to be loved like a child. I am done pretending, I want the real thing." —Dante Bowe

Have you ever asked the question, "Is there more with God than I currently am experiencing?" This question got forever sealed into my heart four years ago. I was flourishing with God, or so I thought. I don't know how else to say it, I was radically zealous for God. I was reading and memorizing the Word of God on a daily basis. I was discipling many people. I was all in. I thought I had encountered all I needed to live a powerful life with God.

Then one night, as my wife and I were listening to Dante Bowe's song, "The Real Thing," we began to pray for a friend who had recently walked away from his faith. As we were praying for him to experience "the real thing," to freshly encounter the presence of the Lord, something inside of me turned, and I suddenly felt empty. My soul began crying out to God, "I want the real thing!"

Immediately I began to converse with Jesus. I pleaded my argument, "I thought I had already experienced the real thing!" I thought back to two years earlier when I had first encountered the experiential presence and filling of the Holy Spirit. Hadn't that been real? I saw Jesus smiling, and then he whispered, "Yes, but there is more!"

I began to weep. I was filled with joy, but yet left with holy discontentment. I said, "If there is more I don't have, I want it!"

The next morning I laid down around 10:30 AM to take an eight-minute nap. I set my alarm and immediately fell asleep. As I lay there asleep, I literally felt a finger touch mine and at that moment, a shot of electricity went through my arm. I jumped up. I did not hear an audible voice, but the thought that ran through my mind seemed as audible as anything, "Can you imagine if I put my whole hand on your head?"

What happened next was the impartation of hunger. I became desperate and lovesick to taste what I had not yet experienced. I read Luke 11 and 18, the stories of shameless audacity and persistence that Jesus painted as an exhortation for our pursuit of him. I began to fast like a madman, days and weeks at a time, asking God to put his hand on my head and baptize me afresh with the "more."

This lasted months, and as time went on, I tangibly felt nothing. I thought, "Am I doing something wrong?" God gently responded, "No, the journey is as essential as the end reward. Keep going."

These months of hunger and thirst, desperately desiring to taste the "more" of God, taught me that the pinnacle of more would never be reached in this earthly body. I thought there was a mountaintop of God's presence I could reach and maintain. I learned His love is limitless and endless. It's a lifetime journey, not an instantaneous impartation. The journey is as glorious as the reward; for without the journey, we would be unable to fully appreciate the final destination.

To be honest, since that day, there is something my soul aches for that I have yet to receive. I wish I had the testimony of encountering what my soul was ignited to long for during those days. But I don't. What I do have is hunger, expectation, and confidence that God is and is going to pour out the "more" over my life. The journey toward more isn't over, it has just begun. Like for me, there is more God has for you; more than you know, more than you can imagine.

"The knowledge of the secrets of the kingdom of heaven has been given to you, but not to them. Whoever has will be given more, and they will have an abundance."
—Matthew 13:11-12 (NIV)

Have I experienced the "more"?

There is more for you than you can imagine, more than you have dreamed, more than you thought possible. God is inviting you to encounter a living intimate relationship. Do you want it? Can you receive it? Are you willing to pursue it? Are there any competing desires that the Lord is asking you to give up? Would you consider laying down a certain desire for a week? What about fasting from food one meal a week?

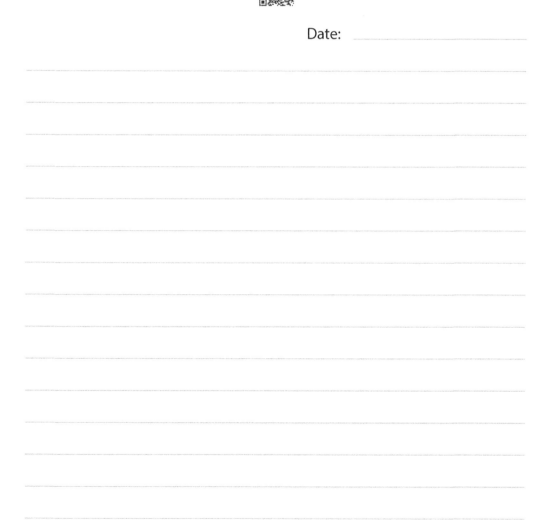

Date: _____

The Heart of the Father
The heart of the Father beats for intimacy with humanity.

For the majority of my life, I thought I knew God. I thought I knew who he was. I thought I knew what he was like. I thought I knew how he felt about things. However, a handful of years ago, the Lord gently whispered into my heart, saying, "Jesse, let me put your perspective right. What you think you know, you don't. You don't rightly know me. And therefore, you do not rightly see yourself." Honestly, I was taken aback. I wasn't living in blatant sin. In fact, I was flourishing with God, at least I thought. I studied his Word for hours each day, memorized verses constantly, and was discipling dozens of people.

Then suddenly, the Lord took me on a new journey. A journey toward his heart. A journey toward how he felt. This was new to me. I thought, as a Christian, I was to study the nature and character of who he is like I would study the nature and character of an influential leader of today. I thought if I just studied him more, then I could apply his principles and values to my life. The way he leads, I can lead. It was like I was reading the greatest leadership guide ever written. But the problem was, I was doing it in my own strength and by my own effort. I thought it was effective. But in reality, it was futile and powerless.

The Lord spoke to me and said, "You are trying to study what I am like. I want you to know what I feel." Maybe this is normal for some of you, but this was foreign to me. "What you feel?" I asked. I thought, okay, I will study what he feels. Then the Lord said, "No, I don't want you to study what I feel; I want you to feel what I feel. I want you to see as I see. I want you to love how I love. I do not want you to study about me, adding concepts to your life to become like me. I want you to walk with me. I will change you. I will transform you. Then you won't have to try and feel what I feel. See how I see. Or love how I love. You just will."

Honestly, it sounded too good to be true. I responded to him, saying, "This seems too easy, God." He responded, "It is easy. You are the one who makes it complicated, not me." I thought to myself, "If it is easy, why do I think it is hard?" Immediately, he said, "Because you do not rightly perceive me. Therefore, you do not fully or freely receive me. You try to work for me; I am just asking you to surrender to me."

This created a paradigm shift in my life. Suddenly, I started to discover the heart of my heavenly Father. I began realizing the anger I thought he had, he didn't. The sin I felt shame about, he had already forgiven. The disappointment I thought he felt, he didn't. I started learning that his heart was full of pleasure. For the first time, I began to feel his affections for me. Hear his thoughts toward me. See the way he looked at me. And feel the ache of his desire to be with me.

I learned that it is not until we discover the heart of the Father and see through his perspective that we can fully and rightly see ourselves. So, do you know how God sees you? Do you know how he feels about you? Do you know what he thinks about you? When I started to see myself through the mirror of the Father's heart, my life completely changed. I started to feel and think very differently about myself.

What I am about to say, I began to feel. Not with arrogance and pride but in humility and confidence. During this time, I woke up in the morning and looked in the mirror. As I did, God spoke to me clearly, saying, "You are awesome. In fact, you are unbelievable. I delight in you. I take pleasure in you." I literally stepped back. "What?!" I replied. God responded, "Yeah, it's true. In fact, what if you said about yourself right now what I thought about you?"

I looked in the mirror and began to say, "I am awesome. I am unbelievable. I am delighted in. I am the Lord's beloved." Since that day, I haven't stopped saying it. At first, I proclaimed it by faith, in timidity, not fully believing what I said. But as I continued something happened. I started to believe. I started to believe I was awesome. I started to believe I was worthy of God's love. I started to believe God wanted to be in my presence more than I wanted to be in his. I believed I was powerful and capable. I became confident in who Christ created me to be. I began to love myself the way he does.

It didn't stop there. I realized quickly that the way I felt about others dramatically changed. The judgment I projected upon people for their mishaps began to dissipate. Relating to people based upon their good or bad attitudes wilted away. The way I was repelled by certain personalities ceased. All of a sudden I began to feel love for those I previously felt anger toward. Those I harshly judged, I suddenly began to feel tender mercy toward. Those I was disgusted by, suddenly, I began to be awestruck over. What happened was I began to see others the way I saw myself, through the lens of the Father. I didn't try to do this. I didn't try to become better in my thinking. More loving in my actions. The perspective of the Father literally changed me. I started to feel what he felt. See how he saw. And think how he was thinking.

I promise you, what we think about God is the most important thing in our life. Our relationship with God directly correlates with our perspective of God. If we do not perceive him rightly, we can't receive him rightly either. Consequently, we will become cold in heart, distrusting his leadership and distancing ourselves from relationship with him. Though we may believe he is real and even that he has saved us from eternal death, we will be void of intimacy today. God wants to restore our understanding of his identity. He is passionately fighting for us to perceive and receive him rightly.

If you agree to go on this journey of discovering his heart, everything will change. When you perceive him rightly, you can begin to see yourself fully. You can begin to feel what he feels about you. Think what he thinks about you. And see what he sees when he looks at you. It will change you, I promise. The invitation is simple: set your heart toward the Father's. If you are courageous enough, look him in his face, lock your gaze into his eyes and ask, "God, how do you see me? How do you feel about me? What do you think about me?" Wait, he will answer. I promise, you will be changed.

"My dove, my perfect one."
—Song of Songs 6:9 (NIV)

How does God see me?

I want you to open your phone camera or go look at yourself in a mirror. As you look at yourself ask God, "What do you see? What do you think? How do you feel about me?" Pay attention to the negative thoughts that come to mind about yourself. Write them down and repent of them. Ask the Lord to replace his thoughts of joy for your thoughts of condemnation. Journal what he says below.

Date: _____

His Perfect Perspective

Your perfection doesn't rest in your performance but in his perspective.

For the majority of my life, I thought I knew God. I thought I knew who he was. I thought I knew what he was like. I thought I knew how he felt about things. However, a handful of years ago, the Lord gently whispered into my heart, saying, "Jesse, let me put your perspective right. What you think you know, you don't. You don't rightly know me. And therefore, you do not rightly see yourself." Honestly, I was taken aback. I wasn't living in blatant sin. In fact, I was flourishing with God, at least I thought. I studied his Word for hours each day, memorized verses constantly, and was discipling dozens of people.

After listening intently to the man/woman in the mirror looking back at you, did you hear the reflecting voice of condemnation declare words like, "You are worthless. You are nothing."? Or have you ever heard the voice of arrogance declare, "You deserve better than them. You are the best!"? The mirror of self-evaluation positions us for two outcomes; both are equally false. First is the reflection of pride and arrogance. It is cultivated by the evaluation that your success makes you great. That who you are is remarkable because of what you have done. The second, condemnation, is a self-evaluating perspective that I am worthless because of my lack of success, ability, or performance. Both perspectives evaluate worth based upon performance, and completely neglect the only perspective that matters at all! God's perspective!

This has been the cycle of my life. Being puffed up in arrogance and pride and torn to pieces in condemnation. Believe me, it is a roller coaster of an emotional ride, filling me with the highest of highs and the lowest of lows. It tosses me like a wave to and fro, giving me whiplash and utter exhaustion. It entangles me in the fear of man. The fear of rejection. And, consequently, empowers me to perform for love, value, and worth.

This all changed one day as I read the Song of Songs. Suddenly the Lord placed me in the shoes of the Shulamite woman, saying, "Jesse, that is you." As I continued to read, I got wrecked by the passionate pursuit of my bridegroom King. I found myself relating with every verse, not understanding why a man with everything, power and beauty, would want me. However, as I continued to read, I realized, not only does he want me, he acts as if he will do everything to get me.

When I began to embrace a relationship solely with him, the need for others' applause vanished, and the fear of rejection was overcome. He took condemnation and crushed it. Then he took pride and plundered it. All that was left was him. It was simple. But it was everything. It was just him and me, which was everything I needed.

The Song of Songs is a powerful articulation of Jesus's heart. It is an allegorical depiction of Christ and us. It is of a woman, worthlessness in the eyes of the world, yet she is of the greatest of treasures in the eyes of the King of the earth. This is my story. It is your story. And, it holds all the power to give us a proper perspective of who we truly are.

"I am dark, yet lovely." —Song of Songs 1:5-6 (NKJV)

It is interesting the paradox we find ourselves in as the one who holds the most power, authority, and influence considers what most people have deemed worthless the most valuable treasure of his heart. This is what the Shulamite woman of Song of Songs articulated when she said, "I am dark, yet lovely." When looking in the mirror of self-evaluation, she deemed herself dark, yet as she got a glimpse of the King's perspective, she realized, "I am the one he wants, I am lovely." Why? She must have asked. Why is my perspective of myself so dramatically different from the one he has of me?

I assume most of us can relate in some way to the Shulamite. I know I can. Why do we see a reflection of invaluable, worthless, or puny while the King of Kings gazes at us with delight, and a deep longing, a lovesick desire for us? Why is our perspective so vastly different from his?

The answer is simple. We were never created to self-evaluate. We were never meant to look into a mirror in which we were to judge our worth or value based on our own perspective. We were created to learn our true worth from the one who desires us the most.

God's perspective is perfect and is not a relative feeling that only he has. It is an absolute truth that determines the reality of all things. His perspective never changes, no matter how much you screw up or how much good you do. Our perfection isn't determined by our actions; it is based upon his perspective. His perspective trumps what we do and is the ultimate reality of who we are.

He looks at you and says, "Loved. Wanted. Valuable. Treasured. Desired. Perfect." It's not until you see yourself through the mirror of God's perfect Son, that you will begin to see yourself through the proper lens. When you do, revelation of who you are will quickly occur. Your self-value will be made whole. Not in arrogance or in condemnation but in the perfection of Christ.

"The Lord did not set His love on you nor choose you because you were more in number than any other people, for you were the least of all peoples; but because the Lord loves you..."
—Deut. 7:7-8a (NKJV)

Jesus, who am I to you?

Declare today, "I am my beloved's, and my beloved is mine." (Song of Songs 6:3.) His perspective is perfect and holds the power to change your life. Remember, you are deeply treasured and desired by the heart of God. Scan the QR Code below and go read the Song of Songs in the Passion Translation. Start in chapter 1, put yourself in the shoes of the Shulamite woman, and begin to let Jesus speak the affections of his heart over your life. As you do, journal what Jesus is saying to you.

Date: _____

My Father's Presence

Presence is most powerful when words are not needed for the comforting of the soul, the encouragement of the heart, or the satisfaction of the spirit.

One of the most profound lessons I have learned in my walk with God is that often I can learn the most profound truths from the most simple people—children. If we allow them, children have a unique way of training mature adults to encounter God the Father's love. It often is our maturity that becomes a barrier to encountering God, as we tend to put up boxes, create preferences, and form theologies about God that are in reality in conflict with God.

Recently I have been learning about God's love from my three-year-old daughter. God has used her to show me where much of my "Christian maturity" has crippled me rather than encouraged me. He continues to be in the process of helping me unlearn the false perception I have had about him so I can learn the true simplicity of his love.

Presence is a powerful reality. It is one God is currently highlighting in my life. As my daughter was watching one of her favorite television shows the other day, I left the room. Immediately, she responded by screaming, "Daddy!" I quickly came back and asked her what she needed. As she continued to keep her eyes glued to the TV, she said, "nothing." So, I stepped back out of the room to complete my task. Again, she quickly yelled, "Daddy!" I swiftly ran back in, asking the same question, "What do you need?" She responded again, "nothing."

Quickly I realized she didn't need something from me, she needed me. I sat down on the recliner as she watched her show. As she continued to watch for the next twenty minutes, I sat in the chair next to her. Not a peep came from her mouth the rest of the time. God suddenly began to open my eyes to see the power of presence. He said, "When you're in the room with your daughter, she feels safe, joyful, and comforted. Your words are not needed, nor are hers. Your presence in her life is powerful and produces a tangible experience inside her soul.

He immediately whispered, "This is like me; I want you to see." My mind was blown wide open, and my heart began to explode with love. For so long, I equated his presence in my life to an hour of devotions in the morning, prayers during the day, or verses that I could declare with words. Simply put, I was equating his presence with words I was speaking or conscious thoughts I was thinking. He doesn't need us to talk to him or actively be thinking about him to be in his presence. He simply needs us.

I began to realize that presence is much more than words, and honestly, it is much more powerful than them too. This isn't to say words are powerless, it is simply to say God's presence is more than an articulation of a thought, a minimal amount of daily time in devotions, or a couple of declarations of Scripture. His presence surpasses articulation and knowledge and releases the realities of who he is in a particular space.

As I continued to meditate on the analogy of my daughter, I heard the Lord say, "I want to teach you to rest in the living room of my heart twenty-four hours, seven days a week." He continued, "I don't need your words, and you don't need to constantly search for mine either. Just be, look, and you will see me."

As I continue in this reality, I have begun to realize that Jesus never leaves the room, but I often do. I routinely enter the living room of his heart early in the morning and periodically throughout the day, but I have yet to learn to remain there. I get distracted by what's outside and quickly run after other things. Rarely do I experience the effects of leaving his living room at that moment; but recently I have noticed how quickly anxiety, worry, fear, stress, lustful thoughts, and despair set in when I do. And rather than mull over these emotions, attempt to vanquish them, or allow them to have power over me, I had this moment of epiphany, "Oh, I have willingly stepped away from his presence!"

Rather than feel condemnation, I saw an invitation from the Father who was standing in the open doorway to his living room, calling out, "Jesse, I am over here!" Immediately I run back into the room where he dwells. I often don't say anything, nor does he. Nonetheless, peace, joy, purity, hope, and love immediately wash over me. I have begun to learn that his presence is my resting place and where I can abide all day long.

"Remain in me, as I also remain in you."
—John 15:4 (NIV)

Are you remaining in His presence?

Have you put God's presence in a box, thinking he can only be encountered when you read the Scriptures in the morning, pray in the afternoon, go to church on Sunday, or meet with your small group in the evening? If so, close your eyes and ask God, "Where am I at? Am I resting in your presence? Or just wandering aimlessly through my day?" Then ask God, "Where do YOU want me to be?"

Date: _____

A Coming King

The return of Christ is hastened by our groan to inherit his glory at the marriage supper of the lamb! The longing for our lover's return is what is meant to motivate our mission with hope and endure our pain with joy. His coming is what will stabilize our passion and increase our love.

I never really thought about the return of Jesus growing up. Sure, I heard the Messiah came and was coming again. But it didn't affect my life or have an influence on my mind. That all changed in the summer of 2018, as God imparted into my heart a groan for Jesus's return and a hunger for heaven to touch earth upon his return.

I was at a summer discipleship training school when a man named Samuel began preaching on the return of Christ. I had never heard anyone teach nor share with the kind of passion he had for this subject. As he preached, he passionately declared the prophetic utterance of Malachi 1:11, "'My name will be great among the nations, from where the sun rises to where it sets. In every place incense and pure offerings will be brought to me, because my name will be great among the nations,' says the Lord Almighty."

I will never forget what he said right after boldly prophesying the nearing of Malachi 1:11. "I don't have hobbies. I have Jesus. I don't think about what I can do in my free time. I think about what I am going to be doing for eternity. I think about his return." I thought to myself, "What in the world is this guy talking about? What are you going to be doing for eternity, thousands of years from now? You think about those things?" To be honest, I thought he was insane. Yet, oddly, it sounded so right. Seemed so attractive. And made my heart leap with longing.

As he finished preaching, he began to minister, prophesying words of destiny and encouragement to those at the school. Sitting right beside me was a young man who caught Samuel's eye. He began to prophesy over him, saying, "I sense God say to you, 'Watch what I am doing. You will be doing it too.'" I wasn't jealous, but I was provoked. I heard the Lord whisper into my heart saying, "If you want it, that word is for you too." Everyone in the room began to rally around this young man, surrounding him with prayers, believing for the destiny that Samuel declared.

As I sat there by myself, I secretly opened up my hands, hiding them behind my legs. As Samuel prayed for this young man, I postured my heart to receive his words too. I said to myself, "Whatever this man is talking about, whatever he has touched, I want that." After he was done preaching, I approached him and asked if he would be willing to pray for me. I didn't share what happened earlier, nor have I shared that with anyone since, until now.

He prayed, I felt nothing, but everything changed. All I can say is there was an impartation from Samuel's heart to mine. Something I had never thought about, I began to be consumed by. I began meditating on the Son of Man riding a white horse, piercing through the eastern gate, coming to reign and rule on the earth. Revelation 19:11-16 became a theme of thought. It became an adoration of affection. It became a mediation of my imagination. A longing for something I didn't know existed leaped in my heart. A groan for a glory I did not know was coming overtook me. In one moment, I was lukewarm and oblivious to the return of Christ, and the next, I ached with longing for his arrival.

Though it may sound strange to many of you reading this, there is an impartation available to you as well. At the time, I did not know what I was doing when I opened my hands after the encouragement Samuel gave to the young man sitting next to me. I didn't know what I was doing when I asked him to pray for me. Later I realized that the reality of Matthew 10:41 rang true, "Whoever welcomes a prophet as a prophet will receive a prophet's reward, and whoever welcomes a righteous person as a righteous person will receive a righteous person's reward."

I received the message Samuel was carrying with a heart of hunger and deep desire. I honored his heart and valued his revelation. I wanted it. Not because I wanted to become just like him, but because I longed to ache for the return of the One he demonstrated this unequivocal devotion to. As a result, Samuel's reward became my reward. Much of his longing became mine. Much of his revelation got imparted into my heart.

Ultimately what I received from Samuel came from heaven. (Jn. 3:27.) It changed my life. It reorientated my focus. It increased and even redefined my love. It can do this for you as well. It is simple, yet profound. Jesus is going to get a Revelation 22:17 bride before he returns. One crying out in harmony with the Spirit of God saying, "Come, Lord Jesus, Come!" Will that kind of groaning be one he finds in your heart? Will that cry be one he hears from your lips? If it isn't, it can be.

> *"The Spirit and the Bride say, 'Come.' And let the one who hears say, 'Come.' And let the one who is thirsty come; let the one who desires take the water of life without price ... He who testifies to these things says, 'Surely I am coming soon.' Amen. Come, Lord Jesus!"*
> —Revelation 22:17, 20 (ESV)

Do I burn with longing for the coming of my King?

If not, open your hands, and spread your heart wide. Ready yourself; God is about to wreak havoc on your heart. Ask God, "Lord, would you make me lovesick with longing for the coming of your Son? Fill me with a heartfelt groan and a passionate cry. Come, Lord Jesus, Come."

Date:

His Jealousy for Jerusalem

Jerusalem's salvation will come in response to the Gentile's passionate prayer for Jesus's unmet desire.

Just as I didn't have a heart for Christ's return, I never understood the heart of God regarding Israel. Obviously, I knew the stories of Israel as recorded in the Bible from the past. But I was void of his heart for Israel in the present. I didn't know he was jealous for Jerusalem or longed for Zion. I was unaware of the blinding that rested on religious Jews, and even more so the discomfort that Jesus ached with as a result.

My blinding toward God's heart for the Jews and his Holy City began to heal in 2019. I was listening to a man named Mike preach on the end-time storyline of the Bible. I had heard, memorized, and prayed Matthew 24:14 hundreds of times. I thought this passage was the key strategy that had to be accomplished before the return of Jesus. "This gospel of the Kingdom will be preached to the whole world as a testimony to all nations, and then the end will come." (NIV) Though true, in my vision of what the mission was to fulfill this passage, I never considered the unique portion of one of those nations, Israel.

As Mike continued to preach, he laid out the drama of the Kingdom of God, and the key role that Israel has had in all of it. That the salvation of the world came as a result of a temporary blinding on the Jewish people. He then went on to say, "One of my life calls is to provoke this generation of Gentiles to be servants to the Jews." Though it was a simple statement, it grasped my heart with great grief.

I realized I was numb to the blinding that rested on Jews. I had no zeal for Jerusalem, and I had no passion to participate in my intended mission with God as a Gentile man. In that moment, I had to wrestle out my lukewarm state and my lack of love toward that which Jesus was gasping and panting over. I had to realize that I had yet to touch a unique piece of his heart and live into a significant part of my destiny.

The days to follow were consumed with devouring the Scriptures attempting to discover the depths of God's heart regarding the nation of Israel. The city of Jerusalem. And the Jewish people. I quickly discovered it is one of the primary storylines of the Bible, and it is one the greatest passions of Jesus's heart to receive his portion of inheritance in Israel. I realized quickly he was returning to the city of Jerusalem. It was not just a historic site; it is the place he will reign and rule for all of history.

As time went on, my times of intense prayer and intentional study continued for Israel. Fast forward to the fall of 2022, and out of the blue I was invited to go on a trip to Israel, fully paid! I was ecstatic to say the least. But I was not ready for what would happen during my time there.

Like I said, I had information, and in many ways had gained an increased heart for the nation of Israel, the city of Jerusalem, and the Jewish people. But what I thought I knew, I didn't as my heart erupted with grief as I walked through the city of Jerusalem and many other places in the nation of Israel.

I realized that the mass blinding was not only on the Jewish people. It was on Gentiles as well. I discovered that 2.5 million Christians visit Jerusalem each year. I also discovered that 1.5% of people living in Jerusalem (900,000 population) proclaim to be Christians. If you know anything about the reach toward getting the gospel to all nations, you know any people group who have less than 2% Christians residing there is an unreached people group. Jerusalem, the city in which Jesus is going to rule on earth forever, is unreached. Yet, 2.5 million Christians visit there every year.

My jaw dropped when I heard this statistic standing in the city of Jerusalem. I was taken aback. God spoke to me in that moment and said, "Jesse, will you become a watchman on the wall of my Holy City? Will you stand on my holy mountain and proclaim my heart over my people? Will you provoke my people to jealousy with your zeal?" Because I had studied so much on this subject, I knew exactly what God was saying and immediately turned to Isaiah 62, "I have set watchmen on your wall, O Jerusalem; They shall never hold their peace day or night. You who make mention of the LORD, do not keep silent, and give Him (God) no rest till He (God) establishes and till He (God) makes Jerusalem a praise in the earth" (vs. 6-7, NKJV)

As I continued to sit in this moment with Jesus he said, "Jesse, the rebellion of the Jews is what brought about the salvation of the Gentiles. But it is the zeal and abundant blessing of the Gentiles' salvation that will bring about the Jews surrender to my Lordship." Jesus continued and said, "For too long

Gentiles have been superior and independent in their religion from my Holy people. You are to be indebted servants to them not separate from them. You have been blinded concerning your role to bring about their salvation"

I began yearning in the depths of my heart. I began to sit on the city walls, take my stand with the heart of God, and start making petition and prayer for Jesus's inheritance in Jerusalem. I asked Jesus in that moment, "Seal my heart with yours. Give me your zeal. Give me your jealousy. Give me your grief." I immediately turned to Zechariah 8:2-3 and said to Jesus, "Place that in my heart."

"This is what the LORD Almighty says: 'I am very jealous for Zion; I am burning with jealousy for her. I will return to Zion and dwell in Jerusalem. Then Jerusalem will be called the Faithful City, and the mountain of the LORD Almighty will be called the Holy Mountain." —Zechariah 8:2-3 (NIV)

As the days followed and I returned to Kansas, the zeal continued. The ache for Jesus to receive what he wants increased. During one prayer time specifically, God said, "Bless them." I thought it was random, but I obeyed. "I began to say, I bless you Jerusalem and Israel." Literally as I did my body was filled with fire and electricity. I knew immediately, the presence of God was responding because of this prayer.

I then began to discover the dozens of passages that exhort us to bless Jerusalem. While I never cursed them, I for sure was negligent to them. I began to bless in this manner because I discovered it honored God's heart and in large part was the partnership I play in seeing the fulfillment of all biblical prophecy. As I continue this journey toward partnership as a watchman on the walls of Jerusalem, I have found it takes faith, effort, and a willingness to push past my world and into God's heart. However, when I do pray, bless, and intercede for the nation of Israel, the Jewish people, and the city of Jerusalem I always experience the powerful presence of God and the deep longing of his heart in an unprecedented way.

I believe if you are reading this, God wants to impart into your heart the zealous jealousy he has for his Jewish people and land. I am sure to many this seems odd. To many, you may have never even heard a train of thought like this. But I promise you, grasping this part of the heart of the Father is critical in our partnership in hastening the return of the Son and ushering in the end of all things. Your destiny as an adopted son and daughter to the family of God is to be a watchman of the Lord on the walls of Jerusalem, blessing the land of Israel and drawing the Jewish people into surrender to their one true King, Jesus Christ.

> *"For Zion's sake I will not keep silent, for Jerusalem's sake I will not remain quiet,*
> *till her vindication shines out like the dawn, her salvation like a blazing torch.*
> *The nations will see your vindication and all the kings your glory."*
> —Isaiah 62:1-2 (NIV)

Do I have Jesus's Jealousy for Jerusalem?

If you have never prayed for the land of Israel, the Jewish people, or the city of Jerusalem start today. Ask God, "Give me your jealousy for Jerusalem and your passion for your people. Bless Jerusalem. Save Israel. And draw the Jewish people to your Son, Jesus." Spend a few minutes journaling to the Lord, asking him for revelation of his heart, and writing a prayer for what he is passionate about. Spend some time reading through and praying the following Scriptures: Isaiah 62:1:-5, Psalm 122:6, Romans 9:3-4, 10:1

Date: _____

SECTION 2
Pathway through Pain

"Son, though he was, he learned obedience through what he suffered." The pathway of Christ to live in the presence of his Father was pain. If the most beloved Son was subjected to this kind of lifestyle as a journey toward his destiny, what makes us think that our Father wouldn't subject us to a similar path? This kind of pain isn't just the outward experience of circumstantial suffering, it is the inner turmoil and tension we experience as we draw nearer in intimacy to our beloved King.

Baptism of Love

"I've never heard anyone say the really deep lessons of life have come in times of ease and comfort. But, I have heard many saints say every significant advance I've ever made in grasping the depths of God's love and growing deep with Him, have come through suffering." —John Piper

I have learned that as you grow in your relationship with Jesus, you grow in a desire to love. The reason for this is simple: God is love. He doesn't just have a character trait or a value system of love; he literally is the essence of it.

In the spring of 2019, his heart of love began to grip mine. At the time, I wasn't even fully aware of what or why I was praying for it, but I would daily ask, "Baptize me in your love." In my heart, I had a picture of Jesus inviting me down into a river, saying, "Let me immerse you afresh in myself." In this picture, as soon as I arose from the depths of the water, love filled every crevice of my being.

Immediately after picturing this scene in my heart, I felt empty. I realized that the reality of what I was experiencing in the above vision was not a current reality in my life. This prayer of a fresh baptism of love exponentially grew. I did not just start asking daily, I started asking every hour, then every minute. It became the mediation of my mind moment by moment.

Eventually, the intensity of the prayer lessened, and what I was meditating on moment by moment for weeks became a dull thought in the back of my heart. However, the passion and persistence of that prayer did not go unmet.

As the next year of my life passed, something dramatically changed that I had never experienced before; I began to feel the pain of rejection and slander, not from strangers, but from people I loved, Christians, of which the majority were friends, pastors, and close acquaintances. I can't describe in words the pain that this onslaught of circumstances produced. I felt unwanted, worthless, and even hated by many whom I had previously felt loved and celebrated by. I felt weak and vulnerable, not strong and courageous.

There was one specific evening after another such occurrence that these feelings welled up, and I began to cry out to God asking him, "WHY AGAIN?"

He responded tenderly but firmly, "Jesse, you asked for this." Left dumbfounded, I responded, "What do you mean? I never wanted this!" I felt his hand begin to cradle me as he responded, "You asked to be baptized in love. I am doing just that. I had to put you in a furnace of hate so I could refine you to carry my heart. You can't truly love until you have felt the weight of hate."

I began to weep. Immediately Jesus comforted me, speaking gently to my heart saying, "This is only a portion of what I carry, my son." I began to weep even more as I felt both the personal rejection of friends and a piece of Jesus's heart being rejected by so many. My suffering with Christ at this moment was producing in me a new level of God's love.

This would be a good time to mention an important truth: Be careful what you ask for, God may just give it to you. Often I ask God passionately for a desire within my heart. Rarely, if ever, does he respond to my request by meeting it with the expectation that I had set. However, he does answer it. Just not within the boundary lines I have set as pleasant.

I thought my baptism of love would come through a powerful encounter that would produce instantaneous joy. However, I learned that often God submerges us in himself by laying a path for us to walk that is very similar to the one Jesus walked. I wanted to be happy in spirit; God knew a better way, and so he made me poor in spirit. I wanted to rejoice with gladness; but again, God knew better. He wanted me to mourn.

What the baptism of love cost me was my reputation, but what I gained was the heart of the Father, the love of God. I'll take the latter over the former any day. I would have never been able to say that had I not walked through the furnace of hate. But when I encountered his indescribable love on the other end of it, I realized it was the richest, sweetest, and most satisfying substance I could ever taste.

The lesson I learned, that if I wanted to love like God, I would have to be treated like Jesus. While the level of betrayal, the sting of slander, and the feelings of rejection may come in varying levels and in a variety of ways, when we suffer for obeying God, it truly is a blessing, not a burden. During these days, God is baptizing each of us in his love, divinely orchestrating events in our life that we would never choose for ourselves, but that are for our best.

Today, embrace your suffering with thanksgiving; God is refining you to carry his love.

"We love because he first loved us." —1 John 4:19 (NIV)

Is My Suffering Immersing Me in God's Love?

Have you ever felt the pain of persecution? The sting of slander? Or the gut-wrenching cut of rejection? If you have, the Lord wants to minister healing to your heart, so he can empower you to love. Take a few minutes to write to the Lord. Ask him to comfort you in your mourning and heal hurts that are in your heart. Then, choose to release your pain to the Lord, confess your anger, choose not to justify your hate, and forgive your accuser. Ask the Lord to fill your places of hurt with the presence of his love. Perhaps, like me, today the Lord would empower you to pray persistently, "Lord, baptize me in your love."

Date: _____

Hope

"Hope is to our spirits what oxygen is to our lungs. Lose hope and you die. They may not bury you for a while, but without hope you are dead inside. The only way to face the future is to fly straight into it on the wings of hope. Hope is the energy of the soul. Hope is the power of tomorrow." —Lewis B. Smedes

Hopelessness is a powerful agent of destruction. It steals away faith and robs us of joy. It leaves us living below the poverty line of what God intends for our life.

I have found this to be true time and time again in my Christian walk. If you have ever experienced a sense of hopelessness, you know the weariness and weightiness of it.

Hope is the seedbed for faith and will largely determine if we flourish in our walk with God. God wants our hearts to be a fertile ground that is filled with hope. If it is, we will live a life of active and vibrant faith, moving toward new places with great joy, confidence, and anticipation. Without hope, we will either live stagnantly in comfort, cower away in fear, or desperately long to escape the place we find ourselves in.

In the summer of 2017, I found myself hopeless. I was desperately longing to escape the place I found myself in. It's interesting that in 2016, when we left for our year-long discipleship training adventure, it was the last thing in the world that I wanted to do. I begged God not to send us. However, as our seven-month outreach phase ended in Thailand, I begged God to let me stay. I didn't want to go home.

However, in his sovereignty, he sent me when I didn't want to go, and he called me home when I wanted to stay. During our time in Thailand, my wife and I lived with four others who were also participating in the discipleship program. We grew closer to them than we ever had to anyone else in our lives.

After that year-long journey, we came back to the same town we had left, and I felt completely empty. I returned home, but it felt like I was returning to a foreign land. I was lonely. I was depressed. I was hopeless.

I wasn't suicidal, but I longed to leave this life to live with Jesus. One day, as I was driving, this newly familiar pattern of thinking stunned me. With deep sincerity and a tender heart, I told God, "I am ready to leave this world. I feel lost. I am without hope. Take me home, God. Let me go in a car accident. Protect my wife. I am ready." It was a vulnerable and real moment for me, as my request to God was sincere.

A few days passed after this exchange with God when my wife and I went to help minister at a discipleship training event. Fortunately, an opportunity arose to express my heart to a trusted group of men. As they ministered to me, what got imparted into my heart that changed the trajectory of my mind was hope. They spoke destiny over my life. Purpose for where I was placed. Meaning in what I was about to do. The simplicity of hope took me from a desire to escape what was next to an excitement to embrace it.

I learned that seasons come and go, but God remains the same. I wanted to return to where I was; he wanted me to move forward to what he had in store for me next. What finally broke down the barrier between the two was my ability to embrace hope and move forward in trust when I simply wanted to let go.

God wants to impart living hope into your heart. If you are cowering away in fear, stagnantly living your life in the complacency of comfort, or escaping with despair the season you find yourself in, God has a gift for you. He wants you to forget yesterday, embrace today, and with joy-filled hope, walk toward tomorrow!

"But those who hope in the Lord will renew their strength. They will soar on wings like eagles; they will run and not grow weary, they will walk and not be faint."
—Isaiah 40:31 (NIV)

Where has God brought me and where is he taking me?

Thanksgiving positions us to hope as it reminds us of God's faithfulness. Remembering what God has done in the past to bring you to the present will allow you to look to God and ask him, "Where are you taking me into the future?" As you meditate on these thoughts and answer these questions, write down what God is speaking to you. He wants to impart hope into your heart so that you can move forward with confident joy.

Date:

Feasting in the Midst of Your Foes

Courage is not the absence of fear, it is audacious trust in God in the face of fear.

The valley of darkness and the sorrow accompanying that place can't fully be depicted in words. We each know this. And though we often intellectually understand God's power amidst Satan's rage, when in the pit of its pain, theory is of no value; only God's presence is.

My whole life, I have felt the weight and reality of "another realm." From as young as five years old, I vividly remember the night terrors that would haunt me. It plagued and debilitated my life with fear. I often would see dark shadows creeping in my window or dream of thieves sneaking into the back door of our house. The dark shadows were more than a terror; often, I would see them while I lay fully awake in my bed. The night terrors that occurred felt more like a reality than a subconscious thought.

As I grew older, the terrors continued. They intensified to the point where I would wake up in the middle of the night, unable to breathe, seeing "shadows" looming in the room. At the time, I was unaware of the realm of the spirit and chalked up my disturbed nights to "panic attacks."

The terrors continued and got to the point where I would feel a literal hand grab my neck, push me into my pillow, and try to suffocate me. In 2018, my nightlife became bizarre beyond belief. I would wake up at night and lay in bed looking out my bedroom door into the living room and see demons everywhere. My body would literally seize with fear. There was nothing in me that could do anything except roll over, cower with my face in my pillow, and force myself to fall asleep. This happened night after night for weeks. To be honest, I was terrified of my night and hated lying down to go to sleep. I would often wonder, "Is it going to happen again tonight?"

As time passed and the terror of the night continued, I heard a simple phrase, "Jesse, stand." I'm not lying; in the moment of fear, I felt incapable of doing anything, much less standing. I felt quite literally paralyzed.

One afternoon, after another terrible night of sleeping, I had a vision. In the vision, I was curled up in a fetal position on the ground, weeping in fear like a little child. Around me danced five demons, laughing and mocking me. Then in the vision, I heard a quiet voice say to me again, "Jesse, stand." I was weak, nearly paralyzed. It would take all my strength to even sit up, much less stand. I conversed with God, asking, "Then what? I can't fight; I have no strength." He responded, "You don't need to fight; I just need you to stand."

As the vision continued, I mustered up just enough strength and stood to my feet. What happened next was flabbergasting. Immediately the five demons that danced with arrogance around me were violently forced to sit on the ground in humiliation. Their mouths were shut, and they began to tremble. I did nothing, but in the moment of standing, God partnered with my obedience to bring about victory against the vicious attack of Satan.

The vision didn't end there. Though the demons sat and I stood, I remained in a valley of darkness. What I expected next was to be removed from the presence of my enemies and brought into a land flowing with milk and honey. However, what did happen was a table appeared before me, and Jesus sat at it. With a smile, he looked at me and said, "Let's feast." I sat across from him and began to eat.

Next, Jesus said, "Jesse, we aren't close enough. Come sit on my lap." Like a little boy with his father, I leaped onto the table and ran to Jesus to sit on his lap. Suddenly he began to feed me. He fed me at a fast pace and wouldn't slow down. My mouth was full, yet he continued to stuff food into my face. The food began to fall from my mouth onto the ground. I looked down, and the demons crawled around like dogs, looking to just lick the crumbs from the king's table.

Jesus looked at me and said, "Everything was created to feast on my glory." I wanted my victory to result in being removed from the presence of my enemies. Jesus wanted his presence to come and camp in the midst of my enemies.

The next night, the attack came again, but this time I stood out of my bed. I was filled with fear, but immediately when I stood, the fear ceased, the demons were subdued, and I began to worship.

I have learned that in God's love, he allows Satan to sift us so he can sanctify us. He doesn't remove us from the valley of darkness, rather, he turns the valley of fear into a river of love. He displays his glory in the face of Satan, not just in the absence of him. He literally prepared a table before me in the presence of my enemies. Lastly, I learned that God didn't need my strength to display his power and love, he just needed me to trust him amidst my weakness.

God is inviting you, too, to stand. He doesn't need your strength to display the power of his love, he needs your trust. When you stand, Satan sits, and God's table of intimacy is established.

Today, even in weakness, stand. God's going to turn your valley into a river and your table of fear into a feast of love.

> *"You prepare a table before me in the presence of my enemies.*
> *You anoint my head with oil; my cup overflows."*
> —Psalm 23:5 (NIV)

Where is God asking you to stand in weakness today?

Each of us have areas of life that feel debilitating. Areas where we feel weak and vulnerable rather than strong and courageous. The enemy is scheming to make you believe that you have to fight in your own strength for your victory. The truth is, you just have to stand in weakness and receive Christ's victory. Ask God, "Where in life do you want me to currently stand in faith and receive the victory you have already given me?" Take a few minutes and journal your heart to the Lord and listen to his heart for you.

Date:

Prophetic Sons and Daughters Arise

"Prophetic companies are a biblical and historical response to the dream of God's heart that every son and daughter would truly know the heart, the mind, and the thoughts of their heavenly Father." —Dan McCollam

I've already mentioned some of the demonic attacks that have plagued my life. I am going to continue. As a child, I was always fearful, and everyone in the family knew it. Whether it was leaving my mother or sleeping in my own room, fear would constantly seize me to the point where I would begin to weep. It wasn't until late elementary school that I would even sleep in my own room.

Strangely enough, I have one night terror that I can remember recurring as a five-year-old child. In the terror, I find myself running around a dusty old city, being chased by a witch, surrounded by mountains. The attack was terrifying, to say the least.

As I have mentioned, these types of terrors would paralyze my nightlife. Keeping me from resting well, living in peace, and living free from fear. Over time I had forgotten the terrorizing nightmares. Still, I continued to be plagued by fear of receiving bad news, living under the heavy yoke of anxiety, and sleeping in fear every night.

Fast forward twenty years. After experiencing a profound breakthrough from the demonic oppression that plagued me in my living room (mentioned in "Feasting in the Midst of your Foes"), I woke up one evening and went to get a drink of water. Not twenty steps in, I was seized once again with fear. I was completely debilitated, as I stood by the window looking outside, sensing that I was surrounded by a demonic presence.

This continued night after night for two months. Every time I walked through the living room into the kitchen, I would have the same fear seize me and see the same thing surround my house. I knew what I sensed was a spiritual war that was cursing my call as a son of God, attempting to manipulate me to bow to fear, and a rage to castrate courage in my life. I did all I could to sleep through the night and avoid confronting the demonic spirit that was plaguing my life.

One morning I was taking a short nap, as I often do. I had fallen asleep for approximately 2 minutes when suddenly I saw, in a dream, a purple pair of shoes walk right up to me. Right away, I knew it was a witch, and fear began to paralyze me. I heard a raspy audible woman's voice violently say, "Are you for me or against me?" She paused for a brief moment before sternly demanding, "AWAY FROM ME, OBADIAH!" Right away, I woke up with the hairs on my head standing straight up.

Right away, I got my phone and typed into google, "What does Obadiah mean in Hebrew?" The answer is "Worshipper of Yahweh."

Next I called my friend Matthew. I told him what happened. Right away, he said, "You have to go read 1 Kings 18 right now." I had no idea what he was talking about, but I opened my Bible immediately. I began reading, learning about a man named Obadiah who hid one hundred prophets in caves during the days of Jezebel's onslaught of the Lord's prophets.

As I continued to read, the Lord clearly spoke to me and said, "Do you read anywhere that Obadiah went and removed those prophets from the caves?" I kept reading. The answer was no. He said, "They hid in fear, and they continue to. Jezebel is the queen witch of the spiritual realm, and she is attacking the prophetic inheritance I have given in Christ. She is wanting prophetic voices to hide away in closets of fear. She wants those who hear me to stay silent rather than speak with courage. She is wanting the prophetic people of God to be chained with the fear of man rather than empowered by the fear of the Lord." He continued dialoguing with me for quite some time. He said, "Jesse, it is time. Rally the prophetic voices to move in courage and freedom. Take them out of hiding, and tell them the good news that there is no reason to fear. In fact, let them know it is time to rise and fight."

He continued, "Remember what she said in your dream? "Get away from me, Obadiah!" Don't run away and bow to her rhetoric of fear; raise up your head in courage and look her straight in the eyes with fierce confidence! Then, begin worshiping. Begin prophesying. Begin blowing the trumpet and sound the alarm to the prophets hidden in their caves. They will follow courage. They will follow my heart. Jezebel will be defeated, and the chains of fear will be broken. The sons and daughters of God are going to receive the Holy Spirit, and they will prophesy unto my Son's return!"

Right after this, I heard the Lord say, "My son, the attack will come again. When it does, weep. It isn't weakness; it is dependence, and Jezebel shudders at it. She is disarmed by your dependence on my presence. She hates your sensitivity to my voice and your courage to confront immorality both in the Church and the world. Don't bow. You don't have to become strong to overcome. You simply have to become dependent."

Not two days later, I woke up, again seized with fear in the middle of the night. This time, I stood rather than run away. I grew weak. My heart turned faint, and I suddenly knew I had two options. First, to let my fear lead to weeping or let my fear empower me to run away. I chose the former. I got on my knees and began to ball my eyes out. Suddenly, fear left, and the presence of God surrounded me. I looked outside, and what I sensed surrounded me before was gone. I felt peace, and I saw Jesus. The demonic presence that paralyzed me was nowhere to be found. I was filled with courage and confidence. I was emboldened and felt called at that moment to take a stand against Jezebel and her schemes. To live my life as an Obadiah, a worshipper of Yahweh, an advocate for the prophetic voice of God, and an equipper of the prophetic inheritance that Christ has given to the children of God.

I began to realize this attack had plagued me since I was a child. The night terrors I underwent at age five were no coincidence. Elijah was a prophetic man of God and was chased through the mountainous desert of Israel by a witch named Jezebel. He was seized with fear because of her attacks. He was called to confront Israel's complacency and immorality. I realized I am called to the prophetic confronting ministry as well. Elijah saw great feats of God, but fear nearly killed him. I can relate to that too. But I sit here writing today with a testimony of victory. Jezebel has not had the last word in my life; God has. She will not have the last word in the Church's life either; God will. God is restoring the prophetic to the Church. He is redeeming children who have been robbed of believing they cannot have access to the voice of God. He is pouring out his Spirit in unprecedented ways, and sons and daughters are prophesying the heart of their heavenly Father.

Why do I share such a strange story? Because the attack I underwent, and continue to in many ways, is one of the primary ways Satan rages against all believers. He partners with a witchcraft spirit that is the offspring of Jezebel to distort the voice of God, squelch the prophetic inheritance we have as children of God, and impart fear into the body of Christ. You may not experience it quite like I have, but there is no doubt Satan hates you having access to the voice of God. He hates you moving in courage as a prophetic child of God. He hates you living with inner peace and confidence. He wants to destroy your courage. Cut off your prophetic inheritance. And castrate you from being able to impart the life of God through sharing a fresh word from God today.

I wonder if you are reading this and thinking, "That's me! I am one of those hiding away in the cave. I hear the voice of the Lord, but I do not have the courage to speak it!" I am here to tell you, today is your day. Leave the cave of fear and step out into the light of freedom and courage. Don't bow to the spirit of Jezebel that is raging in the world, and maybe even within the walls of your church, among your pastors, or your family. Walk in humble love, but move in bold courage! Speak the words of God with confidence and step into destiny to be a prophetic child of God!

"'In the last days, God says, I will pour out my Spirit on all people. Your sons and daughters will prophesy, your young men will see visions, your old men will dream dreams.
—Acts 2:17 (NIV)

Am I fearfully hiding away in a cave or courageously speaking in the daylight?

Has fear from hearing God's voice plagued your life? Has fear from speaking God's voice done the same? Today is the day to come out of your cave of hiding and enter the limelight. Simply say to God, "Speak, your servant is listening." Then ask confidently, "Grace me with courage, God, to say what I hear."

Date: _____

Betrayal

God is the reason why, even in betrayal, I trust, and in persecution, I love.

Can you imagine the life of Jesus? The piercing pain of betrayal he felt time and time again? From his brothers to his disciples and those in his own hometown? Everywhere Jesus stepped, rejection from man was knocking at the door.

This betrayal that Jesus experienced, though temporarily awful, was actually the blueprint for his ministry. It was the expectation he repeatedly set as he explained what it would mean to follow in his footsteps.

In November 2018, I served at a youth conference in Oklahoma. At the conference, the keynote speaker was Randy Friessen, the man who two years prior had provoked me to pursue God with passion. In the last evening session of the conference, Randy passionately preached on the filling of the Holy Spirit, calling people to a place of repentance and consecration before God. Multitudes responded by running to the front, falling on their knees, and crying out to God.

As the worship band stepped onto the stage, I saw Randy slip out and head toward the back of the auditorium. After a few moments, I snuck back to where Randy was and asked him if he would be willing to pray for me. With great intensity, Randy looked me dead in the eye and said, "Do you really want me to pray for you?" Taken aback, I responded, "I think so." He looked at me with fire and compassion in his eyes and said, "It will cost you far more than you can imagine."

I had no idea what he was talking about. All I knew was that my soul was hungry, and I wanted more of God. I responded back, "Okay, pray for me." He laid his hands on me and prayed for me. I felt nothing. There was no tangible feeling or audible voice. I left that conference with no supernatural experience. What I did leave with, however, was an increased hunger to intimately know God and pursue him passionately with all my heart, soul, and mind.

Fast forward two years, and God began to open doors to many ministry opportunities. What happened during this season of life caught me by surprise.

In my mind, I had imagined that when God began to open doors of ministry, I would be accepted and celebrated by the wider body of Christ that I was in relationship with. Unfortunately, the opposite was true.

I began to experience the "cost" that Randy had warned me of. Within one year of ministry, I experienced rejection by those closest to me. The rejection was fierce, and the pain was deep. I heard the piercing words of being labeled falsely.

If I am honest, before passionately following Jesus, being a self-centered, egocentric Christian, I was not only never questioned with concerns for my self-centered lukewarm life, but at times, I was even celebrated. Suddenly, when passionately pursuing Jesus, I became a target for Christians to label me with slanderous and hateful words. I know this sounds extreme, but it's not an exaggeration; it became my reality.

In rawness, I would admit that my greatest temptation has been to dismiss my call to be a fierce minister of the gospel and rather hide away as to not ruffle the feathers of those who were sandblasting me with hateful words. Betrayal has been beyond painful. It has been downright miserable. In the same breath, it has been the greatest gift I have ever been given.

I know this sounds odd, but in God's love, he has allowed me to walk the path of betrayal. As the years of betrayal continued, Jesus spoke to me and said, "This is a gift. I want your joy to be found in obedience to me, not in the applause of man. If I strip away the applause, your obedience will no longer be birthed from what you can get from others, but what you can give to me."

I thought love gave me what I wanted, but I quickly learned it gave me what I needed. I thought God's love would reward me with the celebration and acceptance of others. But I quickly learned that persecution was a reward from the Father's heart of love. Betrayal and persecution, though painful, have been a blessing beyond measure.

Your obedience isn't guaranteed to be rewarded with others' acceptance. In fact, radical obedience to God often will be rewarded with enduring persecution for God. Your zeal will have to bear the reproach of those who reproach God. (Ps. 69:9.) However, know that in the places where you feel the most betrayed by others, is often found the circumstance where you get to experience the loyal love of God most profoundly.

Are you embracing your betrayal with love?

Have you been or are you currently being betrayed? First, write down who has betrayed you. Second, spend a few minutes writing a prayer of forgiveness and blessing toward this person(s). Lastly, I dare you to reach out to them in gentleness and express your pain. With genuineness, forgive them. And with courage, fight for reconciliation with them.

Date: _____

His Heart's Desire
The Heartbeat of Christ is the healing ointment for humanity.

Have you ever pondered the heart of God? Asking yourself, "What does he desire? What does he hope for? What stirs him with passion?" For the majority of my Christian life, I never even considered the fact that God has desires that motivate his heart. I know it seems self-centered to say, but it was true. I was mostly concerned with myself. Even regarding my radical pursuit of Christ, I was concerned with my desires, hopes, dreams, and longings.

This changed one morning as I read John 17 and stumbled onto verse 24, reading where Jesus prayed, "Father, I desire." I took a hard stop; I didn't need to go any further. Those three words deeply penetrated my heart as I heard God the Father say, "You are blinded to my Son's affections and numbed to my Son's emotions. You do not know what dwells within his heart."

God the Father began to speak to me, saying, "I desire to give my Son what he desires. Do you know what he wants?" At the moment, I didn't and responded, "No." The Father said, "You." He continued on, "Do you know his worth? Have you beheld his beauty? Without revelation that he is worthy, you may know informationally what he desires, but you will withhold from him what he wants. Seeing his worth is what will empower you to give him every area of your life." I responded, "I want to know what he wants, God. I want to see his worth and behold his beauty. Show me, Lord."

As I continued to pray, Jesus started to press in, wooing me with the question, "Would you lean into my bosom? Would you put your ear on my chest? I want you to hear my heartbeat. I want you to know my affections. I want you to discover my desires." My heart leapt with longing and love. I literally got flat on the floor, closed my eyes, and imagined myself falling into the arms of Jesus and resting my head on his chest. As I did, I saw his right hand begin to cradle me close, hold me tight, and cover me in love. He said, "Don't rush away from me. Stay here for a little while."

It was in his bosom where I began to hear his heartbeat. I began to discover the ache he lived with, his affections, and the desires that stirred his passion and intercession. I discovered this is where I was meant to live. This is where

I got the blueprints for ministry and was commissioned to fulfill his mission for my life. This is where I gave Jesus what he wanted and discovered just how worthy he was to receive the reward for his suffering.

As I continued to fall into his arms day after day, I was reminded of one of Jesus's greatest hours on earth, the Garden of Gethsemane. I was reminded of Jesus's agony, but I was also reminded of his desire. His desire for partnership. His desire for Peter, James, and John to participate with him in his suffering and enter into the oil press, the place of his crushing. To participate with him in prayer and cry out to his Father. I was reminded that his disciples slumbered and slept rather than persevered with passion in intercession. I was reminded how often I slumber rather than participate in prayer with the heart of Christ.

Though Jesus is no longer in the Garden of Gethsemane, he does continue to live in prayer, in intercession, asking the Father for the desires that dwell within his heart. He sits in the throne room of glory, not basking away, waiting in comfort for someday to come when he can return to earth. No. He sits at the right hand of the Father, groaning like a woman in childbirth (Is. 42:14), making intercession for the heart of man (Rom. 8:34, Heb. 7:25), and asking the Father to give him the desires that dwell within his heart. As he spoke with Peter, James, and John, so he spoke to me, saying, "Couldn't you keep watch with me for one hour? … Watch and pray so that you will not fall into temptation. The spirit is willing, but the flesh is weak." Matt. 26:40-41 (NIV)

To be honest, I groaned at this request. I knew my frailty. I knew my weakness. I felt incapable of participating with Jesus in his request. But suddenly, as I simply confessed my heart, God empowered me in his Spirit. I heard him say, "Jesse, that is perfect. I don't need your strength to complete the task; I just need your willingness to be with me."

I admit, by no means have I perfected participating with Jesus in his suffering or partnering with him in moment-by-moment intercession. But I do know, God takes great joy in the moments that I do. At first, they were short-lived, lasting only a few minutes. But day by day, month by month, year by year, the Lord has changed me. He has transformed me. And now, my weak moments of willingness to simply say, "Here I am, Lord," have been profound.

It is in this place of partnership, weak but willing, that much of what I thought Jesus cared about he didn't. I discovered that the rhythm of his heartbeat was patient, not rushed. Gentle, not angry. And understanding, not disappointed. I discovered that he loved many things that I didn't. I suddenly discovered how to partner with him in the anguish of his desires, patiently praying with long-suffering love.

If you will embrace this journey, I promise you, you will be the redemption of what Peter, James, and John couldn't give to Jesus in one of his greatest hours in the Garden of Gethsemane. If you will lean back into his arms, rather than lunge forward in your own effort, you will discover that Jesus is, again, in one of the greatest hours of his life. He is on the precipice of a breakthrough as he sits on the edge of his seat, awaiting his return. Though we often think the Father would give the Son his reward without you, the fact is, it is you. The Son's reward is and will be fully received in your partnership with him. If you dare to believe, I promise you will receive the desires that dwell within the heart of Jesus.

> *"Father, I desire that they also, whom you have given me, may be with me where I am, to see my glory that you have given me because you loved me before the foundation of the world."*
> —John 17:24 (ESV)

Am I awake to the desires within the heart of Jesus?

We all fall prey to living numbed out in our Christian walk. Numb to Christ's affections, groans, and desires. Jesus isn't condemning you for this truth, he is inviting you to a place of partnership. I have found that simply sacrificing one area where I have the tendency to retreat to find rest outside of him has had a profound impact on my life. So whether Facebook, Netflix, video games, or the plethora of other time wasters we give ourselves to, when today can you set that aside to come lean into the arms of Jesus, hear his heartbeat, and partner with him in his prayers? As you do, journal your experience with him. Write a prayer asking him to continue to draw you out of the slumber and into a life of sobriety.

Date:

Fear of Bad News

"There is a fear of the Lord which is the beginning of wisdom, which is founded in love. There is also a slavish fear, which is a mere dread of evil, and is purely selfish." —Charles Finney

Have you ever dreaded getting that phone call of doom? Fearing the thoughts, "What terrible tragedy will happen next?" If you are like me, it can paralyze you and control your thoughts and actions. For me, it causes paranoia and protective control to the point of manipulation. For so much of my life, I have lived under the bondage of fearing bad news. Always wondering, "When am I going to get a call that my wife and kids have died? When is the news of my parent's tragic death going to come?" It constantly consumed me to the point that every time I walked out of the house or left on a trip away from my family I was convinced that was the last time I was going to see them.

It led me to live an ultra-paranoid, hyper-controlling and strategically manipulative life. I would try to figure out how to live safely so as to avoid disaster. It was causing my soul to decay.

Then, one day as I was sulking, consumed by the weight of the "what ifs" of life, the Lord led me to Psalm 112:6-8, "Surely the righteous will never be shaken; they will be remembered forever. They will have no fear of bad news; their hearts are steadfast, trusting in the Lord. Their hearts are secure; they will have no fear; in the end they will look in triumph on their foes." (NIV) Immediately after I read that the Lord said, "Why do you fear, my son?" My body was literally shaking and my soul was trembling as I knew that the reality of what was written was completely void in my life.

I didn't know what to say back to Jesus. I remained silent and, to be honest, in a pit of despair and a whirlwind of condemnation. I thought, "How will I ever shake off this all-consuming fear? And, if I am not to fear but do, what does that make me?" As these thoughts began to tightly bind my heart like handcuffs, the Lord gently placed me in his hands and gave me this invitation, "Will you yield yourself to my love?" To be honest, at that moment, I had no idea what love had to do with any of this, so I said back to God, "What kind of invitation is that? This has nothing to do with love. I just want free!"

He whispered into my ear, saying, "Everything is a war on love. It is what secures you in trust rather than debilitates you in fear. It is what positions you for dependence on me rather than striving to control your situation."
As the words went from his mouth into my heart, he deposited 1 John 4:18 into my mind. I immediately began to flip through the pages of my Bible until I finally stopped at his words, which said, "There is no fear in love. But perfect love drives out fear, because fear has to do with punishment. The one who fears is not made perfect in love." (NIV) With a deep breath and a desperate cry, I said to Jesus, "Teach me to abide in your love."

As I did, he said, "I will perfect you to abide and bear the fruit of trust and dependence. It is in the secret dwelling place of the Almighty you will see that my ways are good and my protection is trustworthy. The fear you have of bad news is a facade and a scheme of Satan. Under the shadow of my wing, there is no manifestation of fear; there is only an encounter with love. Love, my son, is what will set you free."

I realized at that moment, fear was the fruit of my abiding in lies that came from the mouth of the Accuser rather than from the throne room of God's glory. It was a simple but powerful epiphany for me; the problem isn't my fear of bad news. My problem is I am not abiding in the presence of God's love.

Since then, I have begun to battle for a life of abiding in the presence of God. When fear creeps into the doorway of my thoughts, looking to shake my emotions and empower my will, I immediately declare Psalm 91:1-7, resting my whole life in the hands of this one reality:

"Whoever dwells in the shelter of the Most High will rest in the shadow of the Almighty. I will say of the Lord, 'He is my refuge and my fortress, my God, in whom I trust.' Surely he will save you from the fowler's snare and from the deadly pestilence. He will cover you with his feathers, and under his wings you will find refuge; his faithfulness will be your shield and rampart. You will not fear the terror of night, nor the arrow that flies by day, nor the pestilence that stalks in the darkness, nor the plague that destroys at midday. A thousand may fall at your side, ten thousand at your right hand, but it will not come near you." (NIV)

Though it may just seem like a series of encouraging words, over time, these verses have become much more than that for me. They have quite literally become the key to unlock a door into the Kingdom of Heaven. As I recite these words now, I close my eyes, surrender my heart, and let the glory of God's love begin to minister to my soul. Without fail, his presence begins to wash over my whole body like waves of electricity. With each wave comes a newer level of freedom. A deeper encounter of love. And a fuller trust in the protective hand of God over my life.

Though the fear of bad news continues to creep up on me like a slithering snake, now each time it does, rather than cower in its presence, I rise above its head and crush its attack with the power of God's love.

This encounter with God and the habitual lifestyle of abiding in the shadow of God's love has dramatically changed my life. It can change yours too. If the fear of bad news is debilitating, controlling your mind and emotions, and keeping you in the bondage of slavery, I have good news of hope for you today. A pathway has been paved to abide in the love of God and be fully set free from the entanglement of fear. The blood has been shed, the cost has been paid, and the race has been run. The Lord is beckoning you today, saying, "Come to me, all you who are weary and burdened, and I will give you rest. Take my yoke upon you and learn from me, for I am gentle and humble in heart, and you will find rest for your souls. For my yoke is easy and my burden is light." Matt. 11:28-30 (NIV)

Am I abiding in the love of God?

I want to lead you into a simple practice that has profoundly impacted my life. One of the areas I often fear the most is the death of my family. It has become a routine of mine to close my eyes and imagine the hands of God. Every time they are ginormous. I then picture the one(s) I am fearful of losing. Compared to the hands of God, these people are minuscule. As I picture them, I say these words, "Into your hands, Lord, I give my (wife, children, etc.)" As I place them in his hands, peace floods my body. Trust begins to comfort my fear, and confidence in God's protection supernaturally gets imparted into my heart. So today, I invite you to do the same. As you place your fear of bad news into the hands of Jesus, let him minister to your soul. Spend a few minutes journaling your experience and continuing to dialogue with God about what is occurring in your heart.

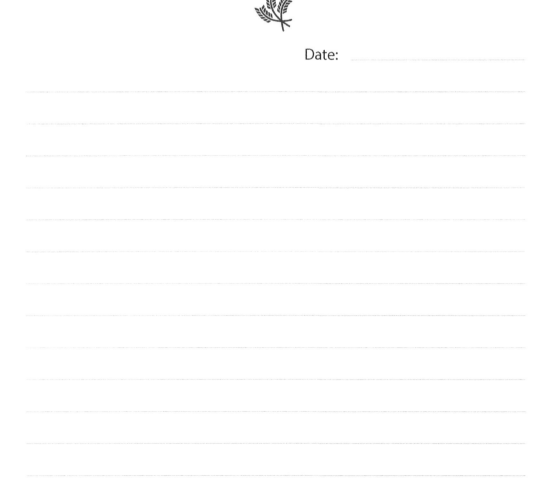

Date:

Surrender

*Surrender is the pathway to encounter, the key to freedom,
and the methodology for success.*

Do you ever find yourself tirelessly searching for any way possible to experience the "more" of God? Asking yourself, "What can I do that I haven't already tried?" If you are anything like me, this question lingers in your mind and is something your heart meditates on. It monopolizes your time.

For me, the question comes with a sincere heart and a passionate desire to know him more intimately. However, no matter how sincere my desire is, often, my zeal for experiencing more of him, becomes the blinders that keep me from rightly seeing the true path I am searching for. Unfortunately, I find myself once again striving in my own effort to get to a place I have no ability to enter into. Because I am so blinded, I think I am on the right path and if I just keep after it, I will find it. The reality is, though, that the thing I am looking to grasp onto has already grasped me. Meaning, the thing I am running after has already run after me, which means I am much closer than I think.

The doorway to abiding in the presence of God is actually so simple that it is profound. And that doorway is surrender. Everything in us wages war against a lifestyle of surrender. In fact, many view surrender as laziness and a sign of weakness. I really believe that all too often the Christian walk is over-complicated and filled with religious expectations that look much more like the law Christ came to fulfill than the life that was slain to bring freedom.

This revelation of God's simple request to surrender occurred to me one day as I was dialoguing with Jesus. I asked him, "How can I go deeper with you and live a life empowered by the Holy Spirit?" Jesus replied, "My son, it is simple, surrender." I replied back, "Yes, I know. But what should I do after that?" With a smile on his face, I could hear Jesus say, "Do it again." Honestly, I began to feel the tension in my body as resistance to his request rose up. I responded to him by saying, "I know I am to surrender, but what am I to do?" Jesus gently rebuked me, "You don't get it, that's all I have asked of you."

As I continued throughout the day, I continued to hear the Spirit whisper, "Surrender." I would respond in faith by closing my eyes and yielding my soul—mind, emotions, affections, and will—to his leadership. As I did, I would ask again, "What next?" I heard the Spirit emphatically respond, "Do it again." So I responded again by yielding myself to his leadership, saying, "Into your hands, I give my soul." Like a small child who is unable to perceive those obvious clues, I responded again, asking, "What next?" The same response came again and again until it finally sunk in: There is nothing else.

When this revelation rose in my heart, I heard the Spirit lovingly say, "Finally! You get it." What happened next was unexpected; I felt like a thousand-pound weight fell from my shoulders. Jesus responded, "You have been carrying a yoke of striving for far too long." I realized that unintentionally, with zeal, I set out to work my way into a deeper relationship with Jesus. Thinking that in my own strength and through my disciplines, habits, and dedication, I was going to somehow obtain the "more" my heart longed for. That is when I realized, I am trying to grasp onto something that has already freely and fully been given to me.

After several weeks, I started to understand deep in my heart what in my mind I thought I already knew, "He needs nothing from me." As I said, I knew what that phrase meant intellectually, but was void of intimately understanding it. Immediately when the thought entered my heart, my love for him exploded at a level that I cannot articulate. I realized it was in this revelation that he needs nothing from me, that I ended up passionately desiring to give him everything, the very definition of surrender.

I think this is what Paul meant when he said, ***"The law was brought in so that the trespass might increase. But where sin increased, grace increased all the more … What shall we say, then? Shall we go on sinning so that grace may increase? By no means! We are those who have died to sin; how can we live in it any longer?"* —Romans 5:20, 6:1-2 (NIV)** I believe Grace is the doorway into the revelation of his love, completely apart from any of our works. This knowledge doesn't produce negligence or disregard sin; on the contrary, it is this knowledge of his grace that empowers us to love him in measures we have no ability to attain ourselves.

Often Jesus asks us to surrender and do nothing so we can learn his pleasure for us apart from our service for him. He wants to strip away Martha-like ministry so that we can learn Mary-like love. Through a life of surrender, we will begin to hear his voice, sense his leadings, and have the opportunity to obey his leadership. Surrender doesn't lead us to a prayer cave where we hide away for the rest of our lives. On the contrary, it leads us to abide in his presence, and be positioned to bear powerful and effective fruit (Jn. 15:15).

A life of surrender values obedience, not productivity. Therefore, if God says "wait," then the most productive thing to do is to be still. Each of us rebels against this to some degree, as we have all been trained by the church to diligently and faithfully work for God, even if we are not working from the power of God. What ends up happening is that productivity becomes so highly valued that it deafens us from hearing his voice, blinds us from seeing his leading, and disables us from valuing obedience.

"All the nations of the earth be blessed, because you have obeyed my voice." —Genesis 22:18 (ESV)

Jesus is leading us each into a lifestyle of increased surrender and submission to his leadership. He is inviting us to take upon ourselves his yoke. It is this yoke that will heal us to hear and so empower us to obey. It will be our obedience to his voice that will produce the blessings of heaven across the entirety of the earth.

"For this is the love of God, that we keep His commandments. And His commandments are not burdensome." —1 John 5:3 (ESV)

The commands of God's voice are not burdensome. However, if we attempt to accomplish these commands in our own effort, they will most assuredly prove to be burdensome and result in burnout, bitterness, and eventual disobedience. But I can promise you that on the other end of your surrender to the leadership of the Holy Spirit, you will experience that the commands you once tirelessly attempted to uphold in your own effort become the very nature of your new life and simple to carry out. It will become the natural overflow of your new creation.

Today, enter into the doorway of God's presence by yielding your soul (mind, will, emotions, and affections) to the leadership of the Holy Spirit. Don't strive for productivity or success; rest in his arms and bask in his love. He is closer than you think and more accessible than you can imagine.

"Submit yourselves therefore to God." —James 4:7 (ESV)

Am I striving for God or am I surrendering to God?

Today God wants to invite you to take on an easy yoke and a light burden. He wants you to surrender your striving so that you can receive his grace to see, believe, and obey. Ask God, "Where in my life am I currently striving for you rather than surrendering to you?" Take a few moments and journal what God shows you. Then write a short prayer that exchanges your life of striving for God to one of surrender to God.

Date: _____

Carrying His Yoke

"If you have God's presence, you have favor. One minute of God's presence can accomplish more than 20 years of your striving." —Heidi Baker

If you are anything like me, accomplishments for God are at the forefront of your mind. For me, my desire is pure. I want to see God get what he is worthy of. I want people to encounter his presence and love. I want to see the captives set free and the blind to see. Ultimately, I want to see his Kingdom come and his will be done.

However noble my pursuit is, I have learned that many of my accomplishments can quickly be demonically empowered. I know what you're thinking, "WHAT ARE YOU TALKING ABOUT?! How can a demon empower you to accomplish work that is for God?" This is exactly what I used to think before the following encounter years ago. Let me explain.

In the summer of 2022, I began to take note of something that had been happening to me for years. Often, right before working really hard for God, I feel a heavy and piercing tension in my neck that shoots up into my head. This isn't a new feeling; I feel it often. I usually equate it to natural stress or anxiety and "push through it." To be honest, the feeling often even empowers me, as I chalk up the anxiety and stress to the natural repercussions of working hard, having my hands involved in many things, and carrying a "big load for God."

Something dramatically changed in 2022. The tension came again. Right when it did, the thought came into my mind, "Yoke of Satan!" I was taken aback. I wasn't consciously analyzing the pain in my neck. I immediately knew that the thought was the voice of God. I responded, "What are you talking about, God?" I heard him say, "This isn't natural; it is demonic. You are taking on a yoke to accomplish for me that which is in conflict with me." I was at a loss for words. "What do you mean, God? I want to be successful for you. How can I be empowered to do so without you?"

There was no response, but immediately I had a picture appear in my mind of Jesus hanging on the cross. At first, I wasn't sure why this picture entered my mind at this moment. Then I realized it was a demonic spirit of religion that empowered the Pharisees to accomplish in the name of God what God was actually wanting to crucify. I was perplexed as to what was happening. I sat there for minutes pondering what God was showing me.

Then I heard him say, "Jesse, you are allowing a demonic yoke to come rest on your shoulders. It is empowering you to accomplish for me what I want to crucify in you." Again, I didn't understand. He then said, "Let me make it clear. You are doing many things for me, but you are doing them without me. You are striving. I want you to rest. You think you are being obedient, but you are actually living in rebellion."

I was sitting at my desk when this happened. I then heard the Lord say, "Turn around." I whipped my chair around and looked toward the couch before me. I saw Jesus's hand extended toward me as I heard him say, "Come, take my yoke upon you; in me, you will find rest for your soul." I immediately stood up and ran to the couch. Sitting down, I inhaled and then exhaled a sigh of relief. Literally, the tension in the neck completely subsided and the pain shooting up my neck ceased. Peace came on my shoulders, and rest began to fill my soul.

Then the Lord said, "Far too often, you are working empowered by motives that are not from me. It's demonic. STOP STRIVING! I don't want what you can do for me; I want you."

I wish that were the end of the story and peace rested on my shoulders from that day on. However, many times since, as I sit in my office chair, I will suddenly feel the weight of a presence rest on my shoulders and attempt to yoke me to religious striving. The tension is painful, and what it empowers often feels wise. Thoughts start racing through my mind, "How much can I accomplish today? What lists should I make of things that need to get done?" If not careful, it will begin to stir me—motivate me. It will propel me forward to write and read about God without God.

Each time it happens, I hear the subtle voice of Jesus, "Come, take my yoke upon you and rest." And now when it happens, I get up from my desk, run to the couch, and sit with Jesus and rest. I give each thought of accomplishing for God to the Lord. I breathe in and breathe out with a large exhale. Nearly every single time, the same thing happens. The tension ceases, the demonic yoke is broken, and the peace of God comes and takes its place. I often hear Jesus say, "Stay here awhile with me. I don't need anything you can do for me today, I just want you."

This invitation is for you too. Do you find yourself weighed down by the need to do more for God? That yoke is heavy-laden and demonic at its core. It masquerades itself with many provoking thoughts that seem to elicit wisdom and guidance. If not careful, it will be what powers your mission and leaves you striving for things Jesus never meant for you to strive for. Jesus is extending his hand to you, saying, "Come to me, my precious child. Let me lead you beside quiet waters and make you lie down in green pastures. My yoke is easy; my burden is light. Come to me, and you will find peace and rest for your soul."

""Come to me, all you who are weary and burdened, and I will give you rest. Take my yoke upon you and learn from me, for I am gentle and humble in heart, and you will find rest for your souls. For my yoke is easy and my burden is light."
—Matthew 11:28-30 (NIV)

Am I striving for God?

Today close your eyes, take a deep breath in and a deep breath out. In complete transparency ask God, "Am I striving in my walk with you?" Sit in silence and listen to what he says. If you hear him say you are, ask, "What am I doing for you but without you?" As he responds, write down what you hear. Be courageous enough to give him your work and patient enough to simply sit and be with him. If you do, he will give you the directives and the power to accomplish what he is asking of you.

Date:

The Way of the Wilderness

Being more than a conqueror doesn't mean a battle doesn't exist; nothing can be conquered without a battle. It means Yahweh wins every time. God takes us to the wilderness to learn that the war ahead isn't dependent on our strength but on his faithfulness.

In my walk with God, I have found that the wilderness is often the way forward to the promise. The question that always lingers in my mind is, "Why?" Why do I have to go through this dry, parched place before I can take hold of the promise?

As I meditated on this question, the Lord spoke and said, "Because, Jesse, if I were to set the promise in front of your eyes today, you wouldn't take it." I rebutted, "Yes, I would; try me!" He spoke gently but directly, saying, "The promise can only be attained by faith, and there is a war that precedes the provision." I replied, "Why is there a war? You already triumphed on the cross! I thought I was more than a conqueror."

As I looked at God, I saw him smiling, and with a slight chuckle and a glimmer of joy in his eye, he said, "My son, you're concerned with the outward provision; I'm focused on the inward transformation. You are concerned with the right now; I'm focused on the forever." Unsure of what he fully meant, I replied, "God, what are you saying?" He replied, "Jesse, I'm molding you into a son who can take over the family business for eternity. You don't even trust me in the short-term. What makes you think if I put you in front of the land I want you to reign in, you would take it?" "But I want to, Lord," I replied emphatically! God gently said, "I know you do. Come on the journey with me. Trust me; I'm patient to grow you. I'm faithful to mold you. We will get there together."

Immediately God led me to Romans 8 and said, "Jesse, you are more than a conqueror! But you think that means a battle doesn't exist. Wrong. Nothing can be conquered without a battle. It means that the outcome is predetermined; I (God) win every time!"

Without hesitation, the story of Israel's deliverance from Egypt was deposited into my heart. I immediately went to Exodus Chapter 13, finding God highlighting verse 17 to me: "Then it came to pass, when Pharaoh had let the people go, that God did not lead them by the way of the land of the Philistines, although that was near; for God said, "Lest perhaps the people change their minds when they see war, and return to Egypt." (NKJV)

As I read this passage, I knew what God was saying. "You're like them. The land of promise is near. But if I put you in front of the land, you will run away in fear rather than forge your way forward in courage. You will choose compromise over trust. You will doubt because of what is seen rather than have faith in what I have said."

God said, "I could wipe the dust of the devil's schemes off the earth with the breath of my mouth without you, Jesse. But I desire to partner with you. All I need is your faith in my power." This took me aback, as I knew I had to admit that I didn't have as much faith in God's power as I thought.

As I confessed this, God looked at me with deep compassion saying, "I've always known your frailty, Jesse. I know your moments of valiant courage don't actually match your faith. Your courage can seem strong, but honestly, you know your faith is weak. I'm not frustrated by it. I just needed you to recognize it before we move forward." I felt grieved by this truth, but also relieved to admit to myself and God what dwelt deep within my heart.

God said, "The wilderness is the way forward, because it is in the wilderness that I shape you into a man of war. I want you to reign and rule forever. (Rev. 5:10) I want you to have the faith to depend on me for the food of promise and for the land of promise. Let's start with food in the wilderness, and there I'll equip you as a warrior to take the promise in the land of war."

It was at this moment that I started to learn that the foundation of life with God is dependence and faith. I learned these aren't nearly as established in my heart as I would like to think. I learned God's way is the best way. I learned to embrace the wilderness, the seasons of testing, and the moments of equipping. I learned God knew what I needed for the journey ahead more than me. I learned that if I couldn't even trust this, I wouldn't ever trust him for anything.

So what about you? Has God spoken promises over your life? Have you chosen to embrace the path of equipping in the seasons of testing, trusting you need the wilderness before you can reign and rule in war? Or do you shy away? Have you returned to the land of comfort? Have you let the fire of passion and the heart of courage melt because of the journey between prophecy spoken and prophecy fulfilled—pain. If so, God is asking you to go with him into the wilderness. He's asking you to trust him by faith for the little, so he can train you to trust him for the much.

Today, embrace the wilderness. Stay steadfast in the season of testing. And you will be trained for the moment of war that is ahead.

> *A voice of one calling: "In the wilderness prepare the way for the Lord; make straight in the desert a highway for our God. Every valley shall be raised up, every mountain and hill made low; the rough ground shall become level, the rugged places a plain. And the glory of the LORD will be revealed, and all people will see it together. For the mouth of the LORD has spoken."*
> —Isaiah 40:3-5 (NIV)

Where is the wilderness God is inviting you into?

God's way is the best way. He wants to equip you for the days ahead. Will you let him? Today, ask God, "Is there a wilderness you want me to embrace? A season of training? A season of testing? Lord God, show me."

Date: _____

SECTION 3
Pathway through Purity

"Blessed are the pure in heart, for they will see God." Your purity is one of God's main priorities. It's not just because he wants you to have better behavior, but more so because it's the pathway to dwell in his presence to behold his beauty. God is on a passionate pursuit to make you pure, singular in love, and intense in dedication and devotion.

Lovesick Longing

Oh, to touch God and still want God is the paradox of life with God.

This isn't a testimony that was; this is one that is. In fact, I am writing this with the groan, the longing, and the tension that I am talking about. I am writing with a lovesick ache stirring in my soul. The longing to be with my beloved and behold his beauty. I am experiencing the inner turmoil of David as he cried out, "As the deer pants for streams of water, so my soul pants for you, my God. My soul thirsts for God, for the living God. When can I go and meet with God?" (Ps. 42:1-2.)

To be honest, I do not know how to articulate in words the desire in my heart that is fully satisfied yet left completely unmet. I do not know how to scribe in sentences the ecstasy of my soul in the presence of my beloved that leaves me undone with love yet longing for so much more. This has been the story of my journey with Jesus. It has been the paradox of his presence and the tension of touching his glory. It's an all-consuming fire of power and intimacy of love. I wish I could tell you that the flames coming off his face and the oil we get to taste in the presence of his grace leaves the space of longing satisfied. It does, and it doesn't. It satisfies, and it intensifies. Sometimes that ache that it creates is more than I can take. To be honest, it almost breaks me.

I thought his love would make me strong. I have found it makes me weak, feeble in my knees, and lovesick in my heart. It makes me discontent, and even at times disgusted, by what used to taste so sweet. Everything suddenly becomes so bitter compared to my beloved. What I used to be awestruck in wonder by in the world suddenly wilted away as waste rather than riches. The obsession I had with possessions and others' perceptions of me faded away. Suddenly, all I wanted was to be in my bridegroom's presence, seeing his perception and encountering his affections.

I know, it sounds cliche. It sounds like Christianese. It sounds like the hymns of many songs that are beautifully rehearsed on Sunday mornings. And, they are just words until they become revelation, then suddenly what was only information actually begins to become transformation. The problem is, I remain in a world that offers me everything I think I need, yet nothing I want. It offers me pleasures I suddenly consider disgusting. Yet, the thing I want most, I can't have.

I presume this will be the rest of my walk and, ultimately, the primary point of all I talk about regarding Christ in this earthly life. It is painfully beautiful. The longing for his love is strangely satisfying. I assume this is what the disciples felt after beholding their beloved for a precious three and a half years, then suddenly seeing him vanish before their eyes. I can imagine that the gift of the Holy Spirit brought them incomprehensible joy, but with that an indescribable longing. Bringing peace beyond comprehension and longing beyond articulation. This is what I feel; it is what I live with.

Christ is wooing each of us into a longing for his return. A longing to touch his face and embrace his grace. A life satisfied in love and empowered by longing. A love that fully satisfies but leaves a longing for intimacy completely unmet is what a betrothal to Christ means. If you want to say "yes" to the best, you are signing up for a life of longing. A life of waiting. A life completely undone by a love you can't yet fully have. It means the right now and the not yet. The pleasure of his presence and the ache that nearly makes you want to break.

Maybe you know this journey with Jesus. The love of your Father and the longing for your beloved. Maybe you don't, but you want to. Believe me, it is worth receiving and surrendering to. Christ wants you to long for him more than you do. This longing can't be mustered up in your own effort. It can't be produced in religious zeal or dedicated disciplines. The groan I am describing only scratches the surface of the groan Christ has for us. The longing he has for us can only be reciprocated by surrendering to the leadership of the Holy Spirit. By letting him comfort you in love but also leave you completely undone.

If you don't yet long for your beloved, simply be still, and hold out your hands. Be careful, he will respond. Say "Jesus, make me lovesick with longing. Stir my soul, and create in me a cry. Make me pant like a deer and be undone like a bride-to-be. Fasten yourself upon my heart as a seal of fire and a ring of engagement, wanting nothing but you." End by declaring, "I belong to my beloved, and my beloved belongs to me."

> *"As the deer pants for streams of water, so my soul pants for you, my God. My soul thirsts for God, for the living God. When can I go and meet with God?"*
> —Psalm 42:1-2 (NIV)

Am I undone by my beloved the way my beloved is undone by me?

Jesus is undone in love by your beauty. He aches with a lovesick longing to see you face to face. The questions is, "Do you ache for your beloved the way he aches for you?" If you are not living with a lovesick longing for Christ, start by confessing to him what has raptured your heart instead. If you are willing to be vulnerable and courageous, open your hands to the Lord and ask, "Would you make my heart break in longing to see you face to face?"

Date:

A Doorway into Intimacy

God rebukes with love, not wrath. He wants us to receive a reward, not retribution.

How many of you love being rebuked, corrected, or disciplined? By nature, our flesh hates it. In fact, we despise it to the point we are repelled by it. Unfortunately, too often, we are so repulsed by rebuke that we do not recognize that it is actually a gift. Many, if not all of us, have probably been disciplined in a manner that has now created unpleasant connotations in our minds. Therefore, the unfitting discipline we received from earthly figures of authority steals away the perfect discipline of our heavenly authority.

Like you, I hated discipline, correction, and rebuke. I would be easily offended when receiving a word of correction from others. I would take a stand against the "harsh treatment of peoples' words." I was quick to defend myself, my opinion, or my lifestyle. It wasn't until the Lord opened my eyes to see rebuke as a gateway into intimacy that my whole perception changed.

One morning as I was with the Lord, he revealed to me the blatant truth that my heart was hard toward his conviction. He showed me how I was refusing to hear what others had to say in regard to my lifestyle, and ultimately him as well. He revealed how past faulty discipline had so wounded me that I had distanced myself from it all together. He showed me that I was decaying in my own opinions and preferences rather than prospering in his.

I quickly learned I had a choice to make. I could continue down my foolish path of self-preservation, or I could embrace his path of loving discipline. The following months involved many rebukes and corrective statements from God the Father. However, I still had a twisted perception of his rebuke. I thought each time God rebuked me, he was straddling me over his knee and giving me a firm spanking saying, "Don't ever do that again." This painful picture only produced in me an unhealthy fear of not messing up again.

My obedience to him in this state wasn't out of love; it was out of fear. He quickly spoke to me and said, "Jesse, that is not me. I am not wagging my finger at you, whistling you over into a private room to give you a spanking. I am gently massaging your back and guiding you back into my arms." My motivation to obey made me miserable. Not only so, but it also dishonored the character of God and grieved his heart.

He said to me, "My heart is slow to anger and abounding in love. My rebuke is purposed for your repentance so I can restore intimate relationship with you, not better behavior." I replied, "Wait, what? I thought you wanted me to be better?" He gently responded, "No, I don't want you to be better for me; I want you to be closer to me. The two are very different." I began to weep, repenting of my false narrative of who I believed him to be, choosing to embrace the reality of who he really is. Suddenly, the fear of the Lord entered my life. But it wasn't the fear of messing up and receiving his punishment. It was the fear of being void of his love. It was the fear of running out of his arms and embracing prison chains in the pleasures of the world rather than resting in the comfort of his loving presence.

"Those whom I love I rebuke and discipline. So be earnest and repent. Here I am! I stand at the door and knock. If anyone hears my voice and opens the door, I will come in and eat with that person, and they with me." —Revelation 3:19-20 (NIV)

If you will listen, God is knocking on the door of your heart. He rebukes you because he loves you, not because he is mad at you. He isn't lashing you with a rod of anger, he is drawing you near with a staff of love. If you will but open the door and embrace the visitor, he has a gift for you. He wants to change you. He wants to reward you, not hurt you. There is a table of intimacy with God the Son on the other end of God the Father's rebuke. If you embrace it, you will learn to be revived by his rebuke rather than repelled by it.

Would you be courageous enough to open the door? Would you be bold enough to believe that God lavishes mercy, grace, and forgiveness in the place where you think he is burning with anger, disappointment, and wrath? Would you be willing to rethink who God is? Letting go of a false perception of a fierce, quick-tempered father and embracing the truth of a dad who is gentle, understanding, and patient? Today, lean into the Father's arms. Embrace his rebuke and receive his reward. Yield to his love; you don't have to run from him; he's not angry.

Is God knocking on the door of my heart?

Are you living in rebellion to God? Are you resistant to his discipline and repelled by his correction? Would you be wiling to listen today? Would you be willing to hear the sound of a knock at your door this morning? If so, would you open it? Would you embrace the man on the other side, invite him into your room, and have an honest conversation with him? If you will, he won't hurt you, he will help you. He will not lash out in anger, he will lavish you with his love.

Date:

Breaking the Power of Porn
God's power can do in a moment what we have had no victory in for years.

I have sat with enough people over the past several years to know that many find themselves longing for a breakthrough in areas they feel enslaved to. I hear a common theme of simply enduring year-after-year, finding small momentary victories but ultimately being enslaved time after time to the same old thing. I have never heard anyone express that they enjoyed their addiction to sin. Rather, I have heard a heartfelt ache for full freedom.

While each person's situation and story is unique, I want to impart hope that the power of God can set you free in a moment from the addiction you have spent years longing for freedom from. While I have many stories of instantaneous breakthroughs with a variety of addictions, I want to share one that many people, especially men, can relate to. The addiction to pornography.

I was in fifth grade when I was first exposed to pornographic videos. It was not long before a little fifth-grade boy was addicted, longing daily to get home from school to participate in this demonic form of pleasure. To be honest, I felt little to no conviction of this sin as it continued to become more and more prevalent in my life. Fast forward a year, and little Jesse watched hours and hours of pornographic videos. For those who have done any research on the effects of porn on the human mind, you know it is quite devastating. In fact, the repercussions to our minds when watching pornography in many ways mirror what happens to a brain addicted to drugs. All to say, my little mind was rewired and severely weakened from functioning correctly.

However, the power of God's transforming grace had a different story. I remember it as if it were yesterday. I was now twelve years old and over a year into my addiction. Seemingly, no one knew about it, and for sure, no one had talked to me about it. I was at my computer when the conviction of the Holy Spirit hit me like a truck. In one moment, I realized how disgusting and despicable pornography was. Keep in mind I was twelve. I wasn't actively reading my Bible or pursuing Jesus. But in one moment, I repented and never looked back. I felt nothing after repenting, and honestly never again thought about what had occurred. However, since that day, I never again had an urge to look at porn. In one moment, the power of God's grace pierced in and set me free from the reign of pornographic sin, healing a mind that had been warped and broken.

"Repent, then, and turn to God, so that your sins may be wiped out, that times of refreshing may come from the Lord." —Acts 3:19 (NIV)

Though it seems too good to be true, repentance is the way forward for freedom. God wants your victory more than you do. He wants you to be set free from the bondage of sin more than you can imagine. We often think we have to run a mile to attain the reward we are looking for. I am telling you, if you move an inch, he will run the mile and give you the breakthrough you are longing for.

On the other end of your repentance is not another chance to be better and do right. On the other end of your repentance is the lavishing grace of God's power, crucifying your old self and establishing your new one. God does not want to cleanse your current clothes; he wants to give you a new wardrobe of righteousness. Today, repent and turn to God. Let him wipe out your enslavement to sin and refresh you with the new life his Son was sacrificed for.

"Repent, then, and turn to God, so that your sins may be wiped out, that times of refreshing may come from the Lord." —Acts 3:19 (NIV)

Have you struggled to be set free from addiction?

Maybe you have asked a thousand times for freedom and felt you never got a breakthrough. Today, ask a thousand and one. Turn your face toward God. Confess your sin with genuine repentance. Open your hands and ask God, "Wipe out the power of my sins and refresh me with the power of your grace." Follow the QR code below and let this song minister to your heart. In the same breath, I have found that walking in the vulnerability of my sin with community is effective in overcoming addiction. Write a prayer to God, confessing your sin and embracing his grace. Then write down one person you can connect with, confess your sin to, and walk in accountability with.

Date: _____

Maturing into a Child

Maturity in the Kingdom of God means becoming more childlike.

Our society values maturity. Colleges are built for it. Employers are looking for it. And most of us are in a pursuit to become it. What if I told you that much of the maturity we value within the church because of the emphasis in our culture, distances us from God rather than draws us closer to God?

I know, I know, this has to be wrong, right? But wait a minute. What if it's right and what we have valued in instilling in our pulpits, pastors, and leaders is wrong? When I became passionate about God and began to discover my gifts with God, I cannot tell you how many people would say to me, "Jesse, you have to go to seminary; you are called to be a pastor!" They meant well, and their hearts were sincerely encouraging me. They only knew what they knew. But, that is the problem.

I didn't know any better, and so I thought, "They are right! I need a seminary degree. I need more training from the teachers of the law, the wise of the world, and the philosophers of this age!" It sent me into a spiral of trying to become wiser, learn more, and find ways to mature in my knowledge. Fortunately, God protected me. One morning as I was reading 1 Corinthians God spoke to me, saying with a finger emphatically pointing to verse 18, "Look here!!!" I looked down and read the following:

***"For the message of the cross is foolishness to those who are perishing, but to us who are being saved it is the power of God. For it is written: I will destroy the wisdom of the wise; the intelligence of the intelligent I will frustrate." Where is the wise person? Where is the teacher of the law? Where is the philosopher of this age? Has not God made foolish the wisdom of the world?"* —1 Corinthians 1:19-20 (NIV)**

I was taken aback and began to evaluate my thinking. Throughout the next year, the Lord revealed to me that the way forward into maturity in the Kingdom of God was to become more childlike, simple, and dependent on him. He showed me that the cross was the entry door into the Kingdom, but only the childlike would truly embrace it. He showed me that the world's wisdom infiltrates the church as much as anywhere. He began to show me that it had infiltrated my life as well. Ultimately, he showed me that I placed high value on human wisdom and considered his wisdom to be foolish.

I chose to embrace childlikeness. But, like anything else, if we are not hyper-vigilant, we will revert to what we know. One day, after a year of embracing the wisdom of God through maturing in childlikeness, I heard God speak clearly to me, saying, "You are doing it again. You are attempting to become more mature for me rather than simply relying on me." I shook my head in disbelief, thinking, "I can't believe I did it again." I heard God firmly but lovingly say, "The moment you mature out of your childlikeness is the moment I will strip the spirit of revelation from your life. If you want human maturity, you will get human wisdom. If you remain in childlikeness, you will live in revelation. One intellectually knows the facts of their study. The other intimately knows the author of their study. The former's office is in the library; the latter's is in their Father's lap. Do you want to hunker down in scholarly study, or do you want to live flourishing in intimacy?"

He held out his hand, saying, "Come with me; there is another way!" I placed my hand in his and haven't looked back. To many, I look foolish. I believe to God I look wise.

"At that time Jesus said, "I praise you, Father, Lord of heaven and earth, because you have hidden these things from the wise and learned, and revealed them to little children. Yes, Father, for this is what you were pleased to do." —Matthew 11:25-26 (NIV)

Consider for a moment: ordinary, theologically uneducated men received such profound revelation that they pioneered the greatest movement of all time, yet the world says we must spend thousands upon thousands of dollars and countless hours sitting in classrooms and attending lectures and seminars before we are qualified to preach and teach the gospel correctly and effectively. What if revelation of God and empowerment from God were on the other end of childlikeness, not man's systems of maturity? In fact, what if our systems of maturing people to lead God's people are actually disempowering them to do what God desires them to? I know this isn't popular and probably is even offensive to many reading it. Don't misunderstand me; I am not mad, and obviously, neither is God. I fall into this trap as much as anyone. But he does have a better way. A simpler one. A more powerful one. One that is closer than you can see and more powerful than you can imagine. If you have not touched it, it will seem foolish to you. You will reject it, ridicule it, and possibly despise it. But, if you embrace it, you will gain a life of wisdom from God, deeper revelation of God, and incomprehensible amounts of intimacy with God.

I thought God wanted my maturity, but I learned he wanted my childlikeness. I thought the mountaintop destination was the growth into a successful man. I learned the mountaintop I attempted to reach as a "mature son" was a figment of my imagination and could only be conquered by becoming like a child. I learned childlikeness was the pathway to his presence and the key to abiding in his love and living by his power.

God is inviting you, too, on this journey of "unlearning." He is inviting you to shed the maturity gained through human wisdom so that he can teach you about the Kingdom of God. He is inviting you to become a child once again. Jesus continues to say to his Father, "I praise you because you have hidden these things from the wise and the learned, and are revealing them to little children. Yes, for this is what you are pleased to do!" —Matt. 11:25-26 (NIV) Reject the maturity of human wisdom and embrace the simplicity of childlikeness. God will reveal to you the deep-hidden secrets of his heart!

"When Jesus saw this, he was indignant. He said to them, "Let the little children come to me, and do not hinder them, for the kingdom of God belongs to such as these. Truly I tell you, anyone who will not receive the kingdom of God like a little child will never enter it."
—Mark 10:14-15 (NIV)

Have I become wise in my own eyes but foolish in God's?

I think at some level we all fall prey to being empowered by human wisdom in our Christian walk. Today ask God, "How do you want me to become like a child?" Close your eyes and imagine a field. Now, imagine Jesus reaching out his hand saying, "Follow me." Ask him, "What hard yoke and heavy burden of human wisdom do I need to let go of to walk with you?" As he answers, choose to let it go and follow him like a little child. Spend some time writing down what Jesus spoke. End by writing a prayer, asking God to increase your revelation of what it means to walk with him like a child.

Date: _____

The Beauty of Mess

What a commission we have been given to be ambassadors of love, demonstrating the lovingkindness and tender mercies of Christ to all.

My guess is we can all relate to the deep desire to live comfortable, orderly, and routine lives. Much of my Christian life has been a pursuit of just that. I wasn't consciously disobeying God or trying to live outside of his will. But what I had unknowingly done was add God to my cookie-cutter life rather than allowing God to be the center of my life. Over the following two years, God began to confront this type of lifestyle. He showed me how I was attempting to fit him into my mold rather than allowing him to mold me. I discovered he came to shatter my mold, like an old clay pot, not to fit in it.

As this process continued, what I discovered was that Jesus loved my mess. He loves engaging and embracing those who are in the deepest depths of despair. He loves entering into the lives of the most dysfunctional. He loves walking with the least loveable. Where we see burden, he sees beauty.

One morning as I was with Jesus, this truth seemed to literally smack me across the face. My soul began to tremble as I realized that I was considering burdensome what Jesus considers beautiful. In this moment, I had a choice to make. I could become offended and conveniently reinterpret the words I was reading. Or I could admit my blindness, die to myself, and let Jesus mold me into what he wants me to become.

I chose the latter. Immediately I was filled with compassion. I was filled with a longing to see captives set free, the blind see, the lame walk, and the poor receive prosperity in Christ. The first words that came out of my mouth as I prayed were, "Give me the ones no one else wants. The situations everyone else runs away from." It was a simple prayer. It was a short prayer. But it changed my life.

Not even a month later, the Lord began to orchestrate relationships for me to engage in that were messy. Previously I would have run from them. Suddenly I started rejoicing that God was allowing me to run toward them. My whole perspective shifted, so did my heart. I saw through a lens of beauty and hope rather than burden and hopelessness. As a result, embracing the chaotic messes of people's lives has become my mission. And though it is often exhausting, I can testify that these relationships fill me with life, rather than drain it from me.

God entered our mess when he came into the world. It wasn't a burden for him. Yet it cost him everything and profited him even more. He came looking through a lens of beauty and hope. God hoped against all hope. He loved against all hate. He saw beauty in what was deserted, desolate, and destroyed. When we discover God's heart with joy, we too will fully embrace mess. We will leave our places of order and our spaces of comfort to serve Jesus in the midst of chaos, anguish, and weakness. Situations will look dysfunctional, heavy, and hopeless. But suddenly, it will be the place you long to be.

The mess of humanity is majestic when seen through the eyes of God. Where you see a mess, God sees a masterpiece. I promise you that embracing the heart of God and the mess of humanity will cost you comfort. But, it will profit you indescribable love. Your embrace of the mess in other's lives is the most precious sacrifice you can give God. Jesus was sent to embrace the broken, and so are we.

On hearing this, Jesus said, "It is not the healthy who need a doctor, but the sick. But go and learn what this means: 'I desire mercy, not sacrifice.' For I have not come to call the righteous, but sinners."
—Matthew 9:12-13 (NIV)

Who can I embrace with God's Heart?

Today, think of one person in your life that lives in a state of chaos, dysfunction, or is just downright messy. Ask God how he is pursuing them? Then, yield your heart to his. Accept his mission. Embrace them the way God is pursuing them. If you do, they will encounter the heart of God, and you will fulfill the mission of God.

Date:

Mediocrity in Marriage

Mediocrity is not what Christ was martyred for.

If you are married, then you know the battle you have to engage in if you are going to flourish in intimacy, love, and friendship with your spouse. Two of the primary prophetic pictures we are given in our natural relationships which depict spiritual relationships with God are found in parenting and marriage. When we discover God, we discover his identity as a Father and thus our identity as a son or daughter. Likewise, God the Son is the perfect husband with undefiled love and eternal commitment. When we discover his "husband" heart, we discover how our heart was fashioned to be like a bride. Because embracing these identities of God are paramount to having the right relationship with him, Satan will rage against these areas in our lives. Satan does not want us to flourish as parents nor prosper as couples.

Not unlike many of you, my marriage is hard. It takes work, patience, understanding, and continual death to self. If not intentionally cared for, time will chip away at that carefree happy romance we refer to as the "honeymoon," and we will find ourselves quickly irritated with our spouse. That fiery undying love is now a flicker, and distance has grown between the two of us. Division has separated our hearts.

Though I have not been married for as long as many have, after seven years, I realize this is mostly a universal truth. According to the American Psychological Association, as of 2022, approximately 40-50% of first marriages end in divorce. And the rate only increases for second marriages. The marriage relationship takes work. As many can relate to, there are ebbs and flows throughout marriage. Seasons where circumstances are great and others where they aren't. Recently my wife and I found ourselves in one that wasn't. I thought to myself, "Why is our marriage so bad right now?" After several days of intense prayer and many conversations with my wife, the Lord revealed to me, "Your marriage isn't any worse than it was last month when you thought things were great. The reason it seems worse now is because I am revealing to you the reality of where your hearts are at. They aren't any worse or better than they were a month ago."

I was surprised by this and needed to meditate on his words some more. I soon concluded this was true. As I continued to converse with God, I heard him say, "Your marriage is mediocre, and you have begun to consider that normal." He continued by saying, "I never intend for you to have a mediocre marriage. I desire you to flourish in your relationship." Again he said, "The reason it seems bad right now is because I am revealing something that has always been in both of your hearts. This is a GOOD season, not a bad one if you will but embrace what I am revealing to you. You need healing, and I have the necessary medicine."

The next words I heard stunned me even more. He said, "The reason your marriage is mediocre with each other is that it is mediocre with me. You think that mediocrity in Christianity is normal. It isn't. I was crucified to give you more than a boring husband. And I am worthy of more than an undevoted, unfaithful bride. You love intimacy with many things, and I am just one of those." My heart nearly stopped, and I was greatly grieved. I started weeping in response to this reality.

If you want to start flourishing with your wife, you need to start flourishing with me, and do this together, as one." God continued by saying, "Together you are my wife. Not Tara. Not you individually. You together. Will you give me your lives together? Will you devote your affection to me together? Will you pray to me together? Will you worship me together? Will you meditate on my Word together?" The truth was, this was not happening. We were self-centered in our relationship with God. Self-centered in our relationship with each other. Therefore, Satan got a foothold. Mediocrity masqueraded itself as magnificent, and we were unaware of the damage that had been done deep within our hearts.

This is probably a great place to address a truth: When you source from your spouse for physical, emotional, and mental satisfaction and affirmation, it is exposing that you are not sourcing your desire for intimacy with God. God is the only one who can truly satisfy your longings and give you the affirmation you desire to hear. If you are not satisfied in and affirmed by God, your marriage will suffer the consequences. You will end up expecting an incapable vessel to satisfy your desires. This will be a recipe for disaster. You will become frustrated, disappointed, and disillusioned in your expectations with your spouse.

I wonder if you, too, can relate. Do you sense the feeling of first love slowly fading and your marriage becoming mediocre in love? I am not just referring to your natural spouse, though I am not minimizing it either. I am also talking about your love for Christ. I am talking about your marriage with the Son of Man. If we are going to flourish in intimacy with our spouse on earth and our eternal husband in heaven, we are going to have to fight to protect our first love. We are going to have to battle for intimacy in friendship and not let mediocrity become normal. We are going to have to throw off all other lovers and be solely devoted to God and to our spouse. We must be able to identify when we need a chiropractor appointment from God, so we don't continue walking with a limp.

Today the Lord wants to examine you. He wants to reveal to you the X-ray of your heart and give you a proper diagnosis of your current state. Maybe the X-ray comes out great. But, if not, do not despair. He also has a prescription of hope. Hope for there to be more in your relationship with your spouse than mediocrity. Hope for refreshment. Hope for reconciliation. If you will take the medicine of hope, you will be able to move forward in faith and embrace the journey toward healing and flourishing in intimacy with Christ and your spouse.

> *"But I have this against you, that you have abandoned the love you had at first. Remember therefore from where you have fallen; repent, and do the works you did at first."*
> —Revelation 2:4-5 (ESV)

Is my marriage mediocre?

How is your marriage with God? How is your marriage with your spouse? The answer to the first question, in large part, will determine the answer to the second? If mediocre, ask God, "How do you want me to rekindle the flame of my first love for you and for my spouse?" Start simple, and begin praying together with your spouse. Share your heart for desiring more intimacy together in your marriage and your walk with God. Small steps can have a large impact if consistently practiced.

Date:

Delight and Desire
God's dreams become our desires as we delight in him.

In 2016, I had a simple revelation from the Lord that changed my trust and my relational interaction with the Lord forever. For as long as I can remember, I have "been saved." I am told I prayed the sinner's prayer at age four. I know it was real and that, at that moment, a little boy received the grace of God. However, after that point, most of my life was consumed by self, and I took great delight in the pleasures of the world.

But, thank God for godly women. In 2011, I met Tara, now my wife, when we were seniors in high school. We ended up going to the same college. During our sophomore year of college, a group from Canada came to campus to give a presentation on a discipleship school they ran called TREK. Tara wanted to go, but I didn't. She won. We went. And afterward, she was filled with excitement. She announced that night, "When we graduate college, I want to go on TREK." At that point, we had already talked about getting married, which meant, "After we graduate college, I want us to go on TREK together." My response immediately was, "There is no way in the world we will ever do that."

She let it go, and we moved on, never talking about it again. Fast forward, during the summer of 2015, between our junior and senior years of college, Tara and I got married. We were enjoying our new life together and winding up our college career, with dreams of leaving small- town life in pursuit of the "good life." Five months into our senior year of college, we get a letter in the mail. It is an invitation to a weekend retreat called The Vision Summit. The flier was crystal clear about the intention of this event. This event is designed to motivate young people to hear the voice of God calling them to live on mission internationally. The organization responsible for this conference was directly connected to the discipleship school that had come to campus just two years prior.

Tara, as you can guess, said, "I want to go to that." I said, as you can guess, "No thanks. Besides," I reminded her, "I have a trip to Colorado planned with a few of my friends for that same weekend." Graciously, she let it go, and I thought I was off the hook. I was wrong. Two days later, Tara told me, "I want to go. I want you to go as well. But if you don't, I will go by myself." I thought to myself, "This isn't good. My wife will not be happy if I do not go." And as the saying goes, "a happy wife means a happy life." So, I swallowed my disdain toward going and relented.

I knew what was going to happen, but I prayed fervently it wouldn't. I kept thinking, please, Lord, do not reignite Tara's interest in this discipleship school! But, sure enough, he did and she was. On the last day of the conference, she approached me saying, "I want to go on TREK next year." I shook my head, saying, "I don't, and we won't. I have personal goals and plans for my life. Going to TREK will disrupt everything." Again, she graciously dropped the conversation.

As the days followed, she continued to share her interest, and I continued to stand my ground. My heart was stubborn. However, in January of 2016, after having another conversation with Tara about TREK and once again completely shutting the conversation down, the Lord spoke clearly to me and said, "If you won't follow me, will you at least follow your wife?" I thought to myself, "I am in trouble. I do not want to go. But if I don't, this is direct rebellion. Not only to Tara's desires, but to God's will."

The wrestling was over, and we committed to going on TREK. I wish I could say it was smooth sailing obedience from that time on. It wasn't. I wrestled in my heart constantly. I continued to dread the thought of going and was frustrated that my plan was now ruined. I knew my plan for my life was a good one and was absolutely the direction we should be taking. I'd even say foolish prayers, asking God to create a way in which we could back out.

One day, in the midst of the wrestle, Bob Pankratz, who led the Vision Summit conference, called me out of the blue and said, "Jesse, I have a word for you. A verse you need to keep in your heart." He went on to give me Psalm 37:4, "Delight yourself in the Lord, and he will give you the desires of your heart." I was both confused and frustrated. I thought to myself, "The desires of my heart are being crushed. God is not giving me the desires of my heart! How will that change?"

Fast forward eight months after all the tension and wrestling going on in my heart, and a simple revelation occurred that had a profound impact on the rest of my life. We were now at TREK and living in Thailand, the place I had no interest in going, doing the thing I had no interest in doing. But in this new season, I was pursuing the Lord with passion rather than protecting my plan and pursuing what I thought pleasurable.

I suddenly realized there was nowhere else on planet earth I would rather be. This experience was the best thing I had ever done. These moments seemed like the most exciting moments of my life. This experience was bringing more pleasure and purpose than anything else before it had. As our seven-month outreach phase in Thailand came to an end, the place I'd had no interest in going I now did not want to leave. My desires had changed because I delighted in the Lord.

I thought as a result of my obedience, I would finally gain those desires of my heart: I would make more money, become well known, and generally have success. But what happened as a result of my obedience was that my desires changed. What I once desired more than anything else, I wanted nothing to do with. And the thing I wanted nothing to do with, I now wanted more than anything else.

I realized God was less concerned with giving me what I wanted and more concerned with transforming me to be like him. What I wanted was what he wanted to crucify, because he knew these were chains that would bind me as I walked out a purpose he never intended me to walk. In his love, he withheld giving me what I wanted and ushered me into a season of learning to delight in him. As a result, he crucified my self-serving desires and opened my eyes to see his true beauty. As I delighted in him, my desires changed. The promise in Psalm 37 was true!

Psalm 37:4 isn't a hopeful quote; it is a heavenly promise. If you will just posture your heart to delight in the Lord, he will both change you and provide for you. He will shape your heart to carry heavenly desires. The things of the world that look good and promise prosperity will suddenly become rubbish. The thing you wanted so badly, you will want nothing to do with. You will end up carrying God's heart for your life. The purposes and plans he has for your life will become what you are most passionate about. Simply delight in the Lord, and he will change the desires of your heart.

Delight yourself in the Lord, and he will give you the desires of your heart."
—Psalm 37:4 (ESV)

Does my heart desire what is in the depths of God's?

Are you delighting yourself in the Lord, trusting him to mold your heart to carry his desires? Turn the eyes of your heart to the beauty of the Lord and ask God, "Open my eyes to delight and mold my heart to desire the will of my heavenly Father."

Date:

An Umbrella of Love

"God loves us not because we're loveable, but because He is love. Not because He needs to receive, because He delights to give." —C.S. Lewis

Love is simple yet complicated. It is desired, yet hard to find. While most relationships require something of you, there is one that just wants you. Jesus. His love is simple yet profound. It is what we all desire, yet at times seem the most distant from.

For much of my life, I created connotations of God's love being a rain that comes under the umbrella of the law. I unintentionally believed that his love was a response to my work. This created a Christian walk of striving in my own strength. Doing more. And attempting to be better. Usually, my heart's intention looked pure, but my lifestyle was slavery.

It is not until I came to understand that the umbrella God is holding in his hand isn't a written requirement of laws; it is in the life of his Son that I discovered the intimate depths of relationship with Jesus I was intended to have. I began to discover that love wasn't a concept I needed to grasp or apply to my life. It was a person who had grasped me, and I simply needed to surrender to. I remember receiving this simple revelation like it was yesterday. When I did, a personal epiphany occurred: "Christianity is the easiest thing on planet earth." I know, I know. This sounds so wrong. I thought so too. It wasn't until I chose to live a life that abided rather than strived that those words actually became reality.

Christianity became simple. It became simple because I realized I was fashioned and formed together by God to have right relationship with God. A perfect relationship. A flourishing relationship. And a satisfying relationship. The information I knew in my head became revelation in my heart. If I would surrender in weakness, I would be satisfied in abundance. It took a lot less than I thought and was much more powerful than I could imagine. Psalm 36:7-9 is what happened to me as I began to cry out to God, "How priceless is your unfailing love, O God! People take refuge in the shadow of your wings. They feast on the abundance of your house; you give them drink from your river of delights. For with you is the fountain of life; in your light we see light."

I began to abide in the power of his protection. Drink from his wine of perfection. And get lost in his love of passion. I began to do a lot less and experience a lot more. I began to abide rather than strive.

I promise, without remaining under the umbrella of his love, we will live empowered by the law, attempting to be more obedient, pure, righteous, and holy out of obligation and duty. We may last a while living like this. But at some point, we will crash. We will burn out, live in constant disappointment, or just straight disbelief.

That which we are constantly falling short of attaining in our own effort quickly occurs if we simply rest under the umbrella of God's Son, and receive the passion of his love, the power of his protection, and drink from the intoxicating wine of his perfection.

It is not a resting that remains stagnant in participation with God. On the contrary, it is a living love that empowers us to partner with God. Under the law, we will obey out of obligation, but suddenly, under love, we will obey out of devotion. If you aren't actively living under the umbrella of his love, you will work for him rather than with him. You will earn from him rather than receive from him.

Today, know Jesus wants you. His love often can feel complicated. Far off and distant. It isn't. It is simple. It is near. It is passionate. He doesn't need you to figure it out or attempt to deserve it by earning it. He doesn't want what you can do for him; he wants you. Your effort will not change you; it will kill you. God wants you to sit under the umbrella of his Son and bask in the rain of his love and find pleasure in his presence. It will be this rain that will take you from behavior modification to supernatural transformation. Suddenly, all that you are attempting to become and do in your own effort will occur in the strength of God's Spirit. Your religious obligation will become lovesick devotion as you rest under the umbrella of God's love.

> "As the Father has loved me, so have I loved you. Abide in my love."
> —John 15:9 (ESV)

How is God inviting you to abide rather than strive?

The same passionate love that God has for Jesus, Jesus has for you. He wants you to let go of working for his love and simply surrender to his love. Today, what invitation does God have for you? How can you let go of striving for love and embrace abiding in love?

Date: _____

The Destiny of a Servant

"Rule with the heart of a servant and serve with the heart of a king."
—Bill Johnson

Jesus demonstrated the life of a servant the best. A laid-down lover committed to the betterment of others over the exaltation of himself. His mission was unlocking our destiny and propelling us to carry out our purpose in life.

I am sure we can all relate to the magnitude of impact that laid-down lovers have when they touch our lives. The people who pour themselves out like a drink offering for the sake of our destiny. They are not only kind, generous, and encouraging. They are life-changing.

I have had many people like this impact my life. Many who have seemingly found their purpose in pouring into my life. I am beyond grateful, and as I meditate on where God has brought me today, I realize quickly it was through the partnership of many servants of God who have spoken into my destiny, poured into my passion, and served my life purpose.

One of these men touched my life quite dramatically from the summer of 2017 into the present time. He is a father who saw in me what I didn't see in myself. Who promoted me to places of operating in my life purpose that I would have otherwise never had the opportunity to.

Growing up, there was one thing I vowed I would never do—be a preacher. I wanted nothing to do with ministry. In fact, I thought it was foolish, and I didn't want to touch it with a 100-foot pole. However, that dramatically changed when a father in the faith, Bob Pankratz, began speaking into my destiny and orchestrating space for me to live into my gifting.

I remember in the first years of discovering the gifting and calling God placed on my life to preach and teach the Word of God; I received countless calls from Bob. No one else was knocking on my door, asking me to preach at their events or minister at their gatherings. But Bob was. Again, and again, and again. To be honest, it was incessant and kind of annoying. But he was relentless.

So, after resisting many times and eventually fully yielding to his persistent requests, I discovered something I was gifted with that I was unaware of and a passion to preach that I would never have imagined I had. Bob saw something in me I was blinded to. He touched something in the depths of my heart that I didn't know existed. He pulled me into a place to live into my calling and fulfill my purpose in ways I never imagined. He used his favor as a platform to empower my gifting so that I could flourish in my purpose. It literally has changed my life forever.

Years after reaping the fruit that came as a result of Bob serving my destiny, one day, as I was asking the Lord the purposes and plans he had for my life, he whispered a simple but life-altering word into my heart, saying, "Your destiny is found in other people fulfilling their destiny. Go low so others can go high. Wash their feet. Become a servant of all. Use your favor to empower others' giftings."

Jesus then spoke and said, "Bob walks like me, do likewise. Your destiny is to be a servant to others' destinies." He continued, saying, "My inheritance is found in my people flourishing in their gifting, living out their purpose, and leaving a legacy of impact. It satisfies my heart, and it hastens my return."

Jesus came not only to save us for eternity but to serve our destiny. The one who is perfect in power, holds all authority, and has inherited the galaxies, is gentle and humble in heart. He washes feet in lowly meekness so that we can rise in confident power. His destiny is wrapped up in serving our destiny.

So, who has served your destiny? Who has laid down their life for your calling? Called you up into your gifting? And propelled you into your purposes with God? Honor them and walk like them. Ask yourself, who has God placed in my life that I can lay down my life for? Whose destiny can I serve? Whose gifting can I empower? Whose purpose can I help promote?

If you will be courageous enough to believe that your destiny is found in serving others' destinies, you will not be disappointed. You will live a life of impact and leave a lasting legacy for eternity. Today is the day to die to your desires of personal promotion and serve the destinies of those in your life.

> "In your relationships with one another, have the same mindset as Christ Jesus … he made himself nothing by taking the very nature of a servant."
> —Philippians 2:5, 7 (NIV)

Whose destiny can I serve in this season?

God places specific people in specific seasons of our life for significant reasons. Ask God, "Who have you placed in my life to serve? How can I lay down my life to empower their destiny? How can I use my favor for their success?" Take a few minutes to answer the above questions and listen to God regarding how you can serve another's destiny in this season.

Date:

Consecrated to the King
Consecration is only religious to the lukewarm.

Marriage isn't flippant, nor is it a lifetime of honeymooning on a beach wasting your years away. It is a journey, one with ups and downs, twists and turns, times of prosperity, and times of suffering. It is a commitment of consecration, setting yourself apart for the one you love. This is the invitation Christ, our bridegroom King, gives. His marriage proposal comes with the expectation of our consecration and our commitment to giving ourselves to him alone.

I like to be strong and spiritual. I love when I'm thriving with the Lord, flourishing in intimacy, and moving in courage with his mission. But if I'm honest with myself and you, far too often, I find myself consecrating myself to Jesus one moment and then satisfying myself in the world the next. I indulge in food for comfort far too much, pray far too little, and am far too consumed with the world's pleasures. This is me. It is my frailty to set myself apart for Christ. It is my compromised heart that justifies my lukewarmness and my obsession with the world, and my longing to taste its pleasures. I hate it more than anything. I despise it with all my soul. Yet, too often, I find myself delighting in it in my time of need. I find myself playing the harlot, prostituting myself, and committing adultery behind my beloved's back.

When the truth of this reality arises for me, I realize I have two options. I can become defensive and justify my lukewarm state and continue to abide in basking in the pleasures of the world and committing spiritual adultery to my bridegroom King. Or, I can repent and turn to God, admitting my lukewarm heart and asking God for fresh fire, passionate zeal, and lovesick devotion for his beloved Son, Jesus Christ. Every time I approach God in this manner, the desire for consecration begins to overtake me. I begin to be disgusted with the pleasures that tasted so sweet just moments before and become fixated on pursuing with passion the presence of God. I began to joyfully throw off everything that was hindering me and the sin that was entangling me and run hard and fast after Christ. (Heb. 12:1.)

I have learned that consecration is only religious and legalistic to the lukewarm. Lovesick brides are not obligated to set themselves apart for the one they love; they are delighted to. The truth is, if obligated to consecrate yourself to your eternal bridegroom King, you are lukewarm in love. Like me, if true, you have to push past your offense and wipe the dust of condemnation off your shoulders. You need to get alone with your beloved and be vulnerable enough to present your lukewarm heart before him. Express your desire for love, but your lack of truly delighting in him. He is better than you can imagine. He won't write you off or sink his head in disappointment. He will embrace you with his love. He will tenderize your heart to his touch with the kisses of his affection. He will give you the power to love, the desire to delight in him, and the longing to be with him. He will take your lukewarm heart and make it burn.

I don't know about you, but I want to live a life of constant consecration. I am done with woke Christianity and a message of cheap grace. I am done with lying in bed with other lovers. I am done playing the harlot and hypocrite. I am ready to journey the mountain of the Lord with my beloved husband. To pursue him with passion. To set myself apart for him alone. To come out of the land of compromise and into the land of promise. To set my gaze on his glory and never look away.

The only thing today that keeps you from a life of lovesick consecration is your denial of your lukewarm love. If you will dare to come before him today in honesty and vulnerability, he will burn up your lukewarm love and leave you with a heart that rages with a fire of passionate zeal for your beloved Bridegroom King. Today is the day to "come out from among them and be separate," (2 Cor. 6:17) fully devoted and radically dedicated to Christ.

"Therefore go out from their midst, and be separate from them, says the Lord,
and touch no unclean thing; then I will welcome you."
—2 Corinthians 6:17 (ESV)

Am I lukewarm in love?

Honestly, you don't have to ponder this question for very long. If you're lukewarm you know it. So does Jesus. He isn't disappointed ready to slap you with the rod of condemnation. On the contrary, he has his hand extended with an invitation. Take it. Spend a few moments journaling your heart to the Lord. Confess your idolatry, repent of your spiritual adultery, and receive his lavished grace of forgiveness.

Date:

SECTION 4
Pathway through Power

The power of God has paved the path for us to abide in his presence. Every event, micro or macro, is in the powerful hand of God working together for our good. Surrendering to his power positions you to walk the path that leads to his presence.

The Salvation of our Soul

Salvation begins at conversion but its ultimate goal is completion. Our soul needs delivered daily from the present age of darkness and filled with the glorious light of Christ.

Salvation is more than conversion. It begins there but doesn't end. The word salvation literally means deliverance. It is not a one-time fix-all card; it is an invitation into a process toward completion. In one moment, our spirit is made complete in Christ. At this moment, full deliverance of our spirit occurs, and we are saved, sealed, and sanctified. However, presently there is a very real part of our being that is being saved. That is our soul.

Our soul is our mind, will, emotions, and affections. It is the place where wisdom, decisions, lovers, and feelings reside. It is the place where much of what we do is decided. Therefore, there is great attack on our soul being empowered by demonic influence and fleshly desires.

For me, the revelation of this reality has dramatically changed my life. I always knew that I received salvation in Christ. However, for most of my life, I was unaware that there was more available for me to experience in the present time than what I was. I knew I needed to be good. Do better. And live righteously. However, I didn't know my soul needed daily deliverance from the demonic schemes, oppression, and strongholds of Satan. I thought I had been saved; I didn't know I needed to be saved.

We are each in a process of having our souls delivered from darkness and transformed by light. This isn't a theological mystery; it is meant to be a spiritual reality we encounter right now.

God wants to come and shatter the strongholds of Satan and set you free to live a life ruled by righteousness, holiness, and purity. He wants you to experience being filled to measure of the fullness of God. (Eph. 3:19)

There is great warfare from this gospel being manifested in your soul. Like you, I have struggled to know how to attain this. How to be delivered from the present impurities that reside in my mind? The idolatry that reigns in my heart. And how to experience the measure of the fullness of God Paul spoke of.

One morning as I was reading Psalm 86:13, the Holy Spirit spoke to me, saying, "Jesse, I don't need your effort. In fact, it is getting in the way of your freedom. I need your surrender." I responded, "Okay, what should I do." What happened next was supernormal but, in the same breath, supernatural. I closed my eyes, and as I breathed in, I said, "You have delivered my soul from," and with a big exhale, I exclaimed whatever thought the Spirit put in my mind. I found myself making declarations of the salvation the cross accomplished that was not fully being fulfilled in my life. For minutes I proclaimed things like, "You have delivered my soul from … anxiety, stress, discouragement, lustful thinking, arrogance, fear of man, etc." With each proclamation, a wave of healing rushed through my body.

As I continued, I realized a simple truth. Less is more. I was doing nothing but experiencing everything. It didn't stop there. Next, the Holy Spirit said, "Any house that is cleaned and left empty is positioned to be plundered. Let me fill you," he said. Immediately, I breathed in, saying, "You have filled my soul with," declaring for minutes statements like joy, peace, patience, forgiveness, humility, purity, etc. Again, waves of glory began to fill my body. I felt the tangible presence of God begin to fill my soul. As I simply sat and participated by faith in the truth of God's Word, the Holy Spirit ministered life into my being.

After months of doing this multiple times daily, I noticed a significant transformation. The situations that once irritated me, I now encountered with peace. My lustful tendencies began to cease, and a pure mind to see women as God does rapidly increased. I could go on and on about the transformation I was experiencing. It was not just a "good practice;" it became a spiritual participation with Jesus in his death while supernaturally beginning to be transformed by his life.

The salvation of your soul is accessible. God wants to pull a future reality of salvation into the present time, manifesting the realities of heaven in your soul. Transforming your mind to think like Christ, filling your emotions with the fruit of the Spirit, strengthening your will to obey, and imparting an undivided love for him in your heart.

Today, stop striving. Stop trying to be better for God. Rather let yourself be changed by God.

Sit down and rest. Close your eyes and entrust your heart to him. As you do breathe in, saying, "Lord, you have delivered me from …" While you do this, let the Holy Spirit bring to mind what he wants to declare you have been delivered from. When the word comes, breathe out, declaring what he has spoken. Continue to do this, letting the Holy Spirit minister to you until he says stop.

When he says stop, let him minister to you with empowerment, filling you with truth. Breathe in, declaring, "Lord, you have filled me with ..." Listen closely, as the Holy Spirit will bring words to mind to declare. As he does, breathe out, boldly proclaiming what he is filling you with.

This may last seconds. It may last minutes. But I promise you, either way, it is powerful and effective.

God wants to unleash upon your life freedom you never imagined possible. In his mercy, he is extending his right hand and releasing favor and grace. There is more for you than the salvation of conversion; there is one of completion. Let the Holy Spirit empower you to encounter the glory of God the way he always intended. Let him set you free from sin so that he can satisfy you in the love of his Son. If you let him, he will pull you out of your pit and propel you into his presence!

"For great is Your mercy toward me,
And You have delivered my soul from the depths of Sheol."
—Psalm 86:13 (ESV)

What does God want to deliver me from?

*After spending some time participating in the exercise above, journal what words the Holy Spirit highlighted. Where does God want to deliver you?
And what does he want to impart to you?*

Date: _____

A New Name

*"God calls each and every star by name. It's not likely
He has forgotten yours."* —Louie Giglio

Have you ever been in a season of life where what you were doing wasn't satisfying? Where work was dull, seemingly meaningless, and redundant? I can imagine we have all found ourselves in seasons to which we can relate.

In June of 2018, I found myself in a season just like this. A year prior, I had come home from a journey of a lifetime, living in Thailand and doing missions overseas for an entire year. Now I found myself teaching at a local high school in the town I grew up in. The job was amazing, and the people I worked with were even better. But if honest, I felt purposeless. I didn't want to teach. I wasn't satisfied because I thought that the purpose God had for me was pastoring at a church, not teaching at a school.

The summer after my first year of teaching, I was in Ukraine, working with local church planters. While there, I was covered with a blanket of discouragement, thinking to myself, "This is what I was created to do; why am I still teaching?" In response to this thought, God quickly replied, "You see in part, but you do not understand fully. Let me show you." I replied, "Great, show me!" But there was no reply, just silence. I was confused; I wanted to know!

Two days passed, and I was talking with my good friend Matthew. I was sharing my confusion and frustration. He responded with a simple but profound answer that changed my life, "You are Jesse, you are created to birth kings for the Kingdom of God." God continued to speak to me, saying, "All vocations are temporary, but you operating in your destiny is eternal." God ignited a fire of purpose in my soul, as for the first time, I began to understand who I was and what I was created for.

At this moment, God gave me a white stone with a new name written on it. Though he simply spoke my existing name, "Jesse," it was as if I had never heard it before. He opened my eyes to my identity and spoke my destiny. What's crazy is that these words from the mouth of God meant everything to me but, honestly, nothing to anyone else. This is what Jesus meant when he said that the white stone with the new name would only be known to the one who receives it.

I can tell you my story, but I cannot give you my experience. Only God can do that. The knowledge he gave me at this moment wasn't informational; it was intimate. It was revelatory. It was life.

I continued to learn that the purpose of my life wasn't wrapped up in vocation; it was centered on understanding my identity and living out my destiny. You may say, "Wait, your destiny is wrapped up in your vocation." I would have thought so too. However, God showed me that destiny is less about what you do and more about how you do what you are doing. There are many assignments, seasons, and works that God has prepared for us. However, our destiny lies much deeper than accomplishing various tasks or living out a particular vocation. It lies within the reality of who we are in Christ and how he has created us.

I realized that whether I was teaching at high school, leading a Bible study with a few people, or preaching to a crowd of thousands that, I am Jesse, and I was created to birth kings for the Kingdom of God. That purpose statement ignited a fire in my soul to return to the classroom and engage each person I interacted with as royalty. It positioned me to live with purpose in every area of my life. It empowered me to fulfill my destiny, no matter what vocation I held or what season God had me in.

The same is true for you. God wants to unveil your identity so that you can discover your unique purpose. When received, it will do something in the deepest parts of you that nothing else can. It will take what is dry and stagnant and make it burning and alive. Today, take your dry place of purposelessness and put it on the altar of God. He will reign fire down from heaven, speaking to your heart, and putting fresh life in your heart.

> "Whoever has ears, let them hear what the Spirit says to the churches. To the one who is victorious, I will give some of the hidden manna. I will also give that person a white stone with a new name written on it, known only to the one who receives it."
> —Rev. 2:17 (NIV)

Who does God say I am?

Take five minutes, and ask the Lord, "How do you see me?" As you do, listen for him to speak a phrase or name of who you are. Write it down and then begin journaling what it would be like for you today to begin living into the identity of how God sees you.

Date:

Nothing Wasted

*God does not waste anything. You are not defined by your past,
you are prepared by it.*

We are each wired with a desire to be great. Though this desire can be twisted, producing arrogance, pride, and self-centeredness, it is an aspect of how God created us to be. My guess is we can all relate to this desire. Personally, not only is it a desire, it is, in many ways, the deepest longing in my life.

At a young age, I realized this desire. I was eight years old when a love for the game of basketball and the longing to be great at it began to consume me. I remember thinking to myself, "I want to be the best basketball player on planet earth." In one moment, a fire ignited in my soul, and I began to pursue greatness by accomplishing the burning desire within my heart.

I am not lying when I say I became obsessed. Many of the things my friends would do, I wouldn't, as it took away time from being in the gym. The food that a normal kid would eat, I didn't, because I wanted my body to be in the best shape possible. I would spend countless hours in the gym, seven days a week, honing my game and giving myself to be the best.

I remember when I was ten years old, a new dream entered my heart. A dream to play basketball at Kansas University. One day I told my mom and dad, saying, "Someday, I will be a KU basketball player!" With sobriety, my mom looked at my dad and told him, "You need to let him know that won't happen."

I thought to myself, "Who is she to say it won't happen?! I am going to make it happen." Whatever intensity I already had ramped up times ten! I became even more of a maniac in the gym. I decided there was no way I would fail.

As time continued on and I entered high school, it didn't take long to realize there was no chance I was playing basketball at KU. I re-geared my goal, as the desire within me wasn't actually to play at KU; it was to be great. Year after year, I gave myself to basketball, letting go of many other things to pursue this one thing.

As you can imagine, my love for basketball fizzled out. The pursuit of being the best basketball player on planet earth never panned out; what a shocker! Those years of pursuing greatness through the means of basketball were painful. I was consumed with others' praise, finding my identity and worth in how others viewed my ability as a basketball player. I was arrogant and prideful, thinking others' success hindered my greatness. Ultimately, I wanted others to fail so that I could be perceived as great. This is painful to admit and sickening to think about. Honestly, what a wretched pursuit!

In the same breath, what a gracious God. When I began to take my relationship with Jesus seriously, I thought those years were wasted! It wasn't until years after basketball was no longer an idol in my life that I looked back on these years and heard the Lord say, "Jesse nothing is wasted in the Kingdom of God. I knew who I was going to make you to be, I began training you as a little child to throw off many things so that you could pursue one thing."

It was his love that let me go down a path of pursuing self-centered, arrogant recognition from others, knowing that at just the right time, he would meet me on the road and invite me to take a detour with him. My desire to be great fueled self-centered arrogance and pride. However, it was that same desire that trained me into a man of intense fixation. Not only were those years not wasted, but they were also effective in the plans and purposes God had for me. When my heart began to burn for his Kingdom, I knew how to throw off many things to pursue one thing. God knew this day was coming, and I can only imagine that he gleamed with joy as he watched my training as a young boy, knowing that he was going to intervene and take what the enemy was using for my destruction and make it be training ground for my destiny.

I thought God was only present in my obedience. I learned he was present in everything. I thought my destiny began when I began to burn for him. I thought he was waiting for me to come to him to change me. I learned he came to me and was present even in my self-centeredness. He wasn't inactive in my arrogance and pride; rather, he was ever present, using everything in my life for his good and mine.

What's your story? Where do you feel that time was wasted? God wants to bring you to a higher place and see from a more perfect perspective. Your past not only isn't wasted, if you will embrace it, it was training ground for you to walk in authority, power, and passion with God in your destiny. God has longsuffered with steadfast love throughout all of our life. He hasn't left us, nor has he ignored our story. Rather, he is shaping it, using it, and wanting to enhance it for the greatness of his Kingdom. In response, rejoice for yesterday, embrace today, and let them both propel you into your destiny tomorrow!

"And we know that in all things God works for the good of those who love him, who have been called according to his purpose."
—Romans 8:28 (NIV)

How has my past trained me for the present?

Often we try to forget yesterday's misplaced passions. While not dwelling in condemnation on them is critical, recognizing that God was using them is just as essential. What past misplaced passion(s) has God used as training ground in your life for your destiny with him? Spend some time reminiscing with God, asking him, "God where in my life have I considered something wasted that you have actually used for my good?"

Date: _____

Son of Inheritance

Ceilings become floors when you live for the Kingdom of God.

One of the greatest blessings I have ever received is the leadership of "spiritual fathers." When I began to passionately pursue Jesus, I was surrounded by men who deeply loved God, intimately knew God, and powerfully walked with God. These men were not just mentors; they quickly became fathers. They tenderly cared for my heart. They lovingly rebuked my actions. And they passionately poured into my calling. They empowered me. They believed in me. And they sent me.

These four men changed my life. However, it was interesting; as time progressed, I discovered that both gratitude and reverence can quickly subside. In fact, one of the primary tactics of the devil is to disarm honor from the sons of God so that they walk in jealousy of others and arrogance in themselves. When this happens, we reject the God-given gift that God graciously places in our life. Rather than receive another in the name of what they are called, we despise what God has called them.

This has happened to me. One afternoon as I was sitting in my office, God spoke to me and said, "You have been blinded to what you have been given. You have lost honor and appreciation for your fathers. You have normalized their presence in your life to the point that no longer are you hungry to receive; in fact you're jealous of what they carry." Whoa, I thought. What a rebuke. It didn't take long to admit that what God spoke resided in my heart.

At first, I was devastated. Why would I be jealous of those who have believed in me the most? But if honest, I was. It didn't start this way. When I met them all, I not only appreciated them, I sincerely wanted what they carried out of godly hunger, not fleshly jealousy. But what started with childlike receptivity quickly became brotherly competition. In my heart, I no longer honored them as fathers or loved them as blessed brothers. Rather, a spirit of comparison and competitiveness was allowed access to my heart. The men I had humbly asked to lay hands on me and pray every time I saw them became the same men I arrogantly compared myself with.

I discovered many things during this season. First, honor is worth protecting and therefore hated by Satan. He maliciously attacks honor in each of our lives. Wanting to make childlike sons arrogant men. Secondly, If you can't receive what a father carries in humility, you will never be able to give a son what you carry generously. Both jealousy and pride will eat you alive. I promise you, if anything like me, there is a great attack on you being a son of inheritance and a father of blessing.

God wants to break off of you the orphan spirit of jealousy and pride. He wants you to serve humbly so that you can lead confidently. You have to be humble enough to say, "I don't know, teach me," before you can confidently say, "I know, let me teach you." Both are cyclical. Meaning you don't graduate out of the former and then become an expert in the latter. When you live in the power of meekness, you will love to learn from others as much as you love to lead others. Therefore, you will constantly interact with others by saying both, "I don't know, teach me" and "I know, let me teach you."

God wants to impart spiritual fathers/mothers into your life. He wants you to humbly serve so that their ceiling can become your floor. If you embrace being a son/daughter of blessing, God will raise you up to be a father/mother of inheritance. He will make you both humble to receive and confident to lead. He will mold you into a servant and raise you up as a king. Consequently, your ceiling will become the next generation's floor. You will consequently father/mother with the heart of a servant, freely and generously giving to sons and daughters what was given to you.

> "Even if you had ten thousand guardians in Christ, you do not have many fathers, for in Christ Jesus I became your father through the gospel."
> —1 Corinthians 4:15 (NIV)

Am I receiving others in the name of what God has called them?

What gifts has God given you in people? Ask yourself, "Who does God call these people? And, how can I honor these people?" If you are willing to humbly honor them as a gift rather than compete against them as an opponent, God has a gift of impartation he wants to give you. Today, spend a few minutes identifying the gifts God has given you in people and how you could walk in honor and receptivity to what they carry with Christ.

Date:

Discovering the Will of God

"Being a Christian is less about cautiously avoiding sin than about courageously and actively doing God's will." —Deitrich Bonhoeffer

If you're anything like me, you know the tension that exists inwardly in attempting to discover and obey the will of God. Often, hearing the phrase "God's will" is weighty and lofty. It can quickly become overwhelming and intimidating. In the same breath, it is clearly critical to seek to discover if we are going to live a life of obedience to God. (See Eph. 5:17, Rom. 12:2, Jn. 7:17, Heb. 10:36, 13:20-21.) So, how do we discover the will of God without being weighed down by massive intimidation?

Recently I have been on a passionate and lovesick pursuit to discover the will of God. This pursuit began with a simple but powerful discovery that God opened my eyes to. While studying Matthew 6:10, I meditated intentionally on the phrase "your will be done." I discovered that the Greek word "will" could be translated to "desire." Meaning we could pray, "your kingdom come, your desire be done, on earth as it is in heaven." Then the Lord immediately asked me, "Where do desires lie?" I responded, "In the heart." God said, "Exactly, you are on a pursuit to discover the desires that lie within my heart."

He then asked me, "How do you discover desires that lie within a person's heart?" I took a minute to think, and then it hit me, "Intimate friendship!" He responded with excitement, "YES, my dear friend, intimacy is the key to discovering the desires within my heart!" This simple conversation with God birthed new levels of faith within me, believing with confidence that I could know the will of God and the desires that lie within his heart.

As weeks passed and I passionately began to pursue the depths of God's heart in a new way, the Lord prompted me to begin meditating on the life of Jesus and his pursuit of discovering his Father's will. I began to realize the rhythms of Jesus's life in a new way, seeing how he carved out his early morning and late evening to be in intimate communion with his Father before executing his ministry for his Father. (See Mk. 1:35, Lk. 6:12.) This brought up many questions: "Why did Jesus do this? Was he not God? Did he not know all things?"

As I continued meditating on this, I began to wonder, what was communion with the Father like for Jesus? Did he hear an audible voice or receive his specific assignments for every moment of the day? Or, was his time with the Father like our time with the Father? Did he meditate on the Scriptures? Did he sit in silence and listen for the "still small voice"? Or, like we are exhorted to, did he simply stay radically committed and consistent with seeking his Father faithfully day-by-day? As a result of a steadfast pursuit of discovering his Father's will, did Jesus grow in intimate knowledge of the desires in his Father's heart and learn to faithfully obey what his Father wanted? I believe so. (See Lk. 2:52, Heb. 5:8.)

Jesus was the normal expression of what Christianity is meant to look like. He is perfect theology and the model or measure we are meant to evaluate our life by. (See 1 Jn. 2:5-6.) Though we will not attain the perfection or Godhead of Christ, this intimate walk with the Father is the invitation each of us is invited into as well. I believe Jesus's discovery of the desires that lay within the Father's heart was supernaturally normal. Meaning, Jesus sought and discovered the will of the Father the same way we are invited to.

"Very truly I tell you, the Son can do nothing by himself; he can do only what he sees his Father doing, because whatever the Father does the Son also does." —John 5:19 (NIV)

I believe Jesus walked by faith, not with an earbud that was bluetoothed to the audible voice of God. Like any intimate relationship, Jesus had discovered his lover's heart and knew what brought the Father pleasure and what he would desire within any given situation. He knew that his Father was good and a giver of life. Therefore, wherever destruction, death, and theft were present, he knew his Father's heart was grieved. As a result, he walked as a conduit to his Father's heart, releasing healing, life, and redemption (Jn. 10:10).

Discovering the desires within the Father's heart is possible, and more so, is your destiny. Intimacy is the doorway into discovery and will produce in you revelation of what the Father wants and is worthy of. As a result of this discovery, you will be both aware and empowered to be the conduit of the Father's heart, releasing life, healing, and redemption in every situation you encounter. (See Jn. 14:12-14.) Like Jesus we too can declare, "I am a son of the Most High God. I can do nothing by myself, but I have begun to discover the desire of my Father's heart; thus, I do only what I see him doing, because whatever the Father does, I do also."

How does God want me to discover the desires within his heart?

Are you pursuing Christ faithfully and staying steadfast daily? If not, God has an invitation for you today. An invitation to intimacy. An invitation to friendship. An invitation to discovery. How can you begin to allow Christ to be the cornerstone of your life rather than a secondary thought in your life? Today ask God to give you a Scripture. Write it below and then converse with God asking him, "Lord, what is the desire within your heart that you want to put in mine?"

Date:

Manna to my Soul

"The words of Scripture thrill my soul as nothing else ever can. They bear me aloft or dash me down. They tear me in pieces or build me up. The words of God have more power over me than ever David's fingers had over his harp strings. IS it not so with you?" —Charles Spurgeon

In the spring of 2018, I had a profound epiphany that would change the trajectory of my walk with Christ dramatically. One morning while I was reading Scripture, I came across Joshua 1:8: "Keep this book of the law on your lips, meditate on it day and night so that you may be careful to do everything written in it. Then you will be prosperous and successful." Immediately I was dumbfounded as the simplicity of prosperity, and success stood right before me. Initially, as I read that verse, I began to meditate on two questions: 1) What are prosperity and success in the Kingdom of God, and 2) How do I attain that prosperity on earth as it is in heaven? It seemed plain as day, to begin to keep the Word of God on my lips, meditating on it day and night. So, I did just that, and the journey of tattooing the Word of God on my heart with fervent zeal began.

I quickly realized that his Word was a substance of truth that supernaturally empowered change in my life. As days passed and his words became more engrained in my heart, I began to realize they were more than words. They were more than good teachings. They were more than commands that I should apply to my life. I began to discover they were active, living, breathing, and alive. I started to experience them like oxygen that I breathe, blood that flows through my veins, and water that I drink. They literally started to transform me. I began to think differently. My heart began to feel differently. And my will began to act differently. Honestly, the difference I noticed wasn't because of my good behavior or my radical intentionality to be better for God. It was as if God's words were a surgical scalpel, and with each one I read cancer was being removed from my body. My soul started to flourish. My mind began to be pure. My emotions began to live in peace. My will began to naturally obey. And my heart began to radically love.

I didn't try to think better; I just did. I didn't try to love more purely; it just happened. I didn't try to live a more holy life; again, it just happened. His Word pierced me. It crucified me. It resurrected me. It transformed me. And it continues to today.

During this season of life, memorizing and meditating on the Word of God wasn't a discipline I did to earn God's love. It was a passion I had because I abided in his love. It wasn't me attempting to earn something; it was an active relationship of me receiving everything.

I learned I wasn't meditating on Scripture for others or even for me; I was memorizing and meditating on it for him. What I mean is that his words literally became an agent of change in my life and began to transform me into the man Christ was sacrificed to receive. Rather than merely being a means to preaching eloquently or even to personally experiencing the blessings of heaven because of living righteously, the Word became a means toward Christ receiving his inheritance in me.

I often hear people tell me, "I could never memorize Scripture like you." I know they mean well, but I do not believe that it is true. Whether it is one passage of Scripture or a thousand, God is inviting each of us to meditate on his Word with passion and memorize it with great intensity. He's inviting you to tattoo his Word into your mind and hide them within your heart.

He is inviting you to feast on his Word, take fascination in his wisdom, and bask in his revelation. It is more than good teachings, it is a pathway into his presence and bread to your soul. Like he exhorted Joshua, he is exhorting you. Today, God is inviting you into a life of obedience, prosperity, and blessing. He is inviting you to come to his dinner table of feasting and the surgery table of transformation. He wants you to eat of him so that you can become like him.

Today is the day to take hold of heaven. If God's words are bitter not sweet and boring not beautiful to you, don't be disappointed or discouraged. Mount up in faith and simply begin to meditate on his Word. Keep it on your lips and meditate on it within your heart. I promise, if you do, God will take what was once boring and make it beautiful, what was once bitter and make it sweet. He will satisfy your soul and change your heart.

> *"Jesus answered, "It is written: 'Man shall not live on bread alone,*
> *but on every word that comes from the mouth of God.'"*
> *—Matthew 4:4 (NIV)*

Is God's Word growing in me like a seed?

Small seeds become big trees when they are tended to with care and intentionality. God is inviting you to open up his Word, and pick one of the 31,102 seeds (the number of verses that are in the Bible) today. He will specifically lead you to the one he knows you need. If you partner with him in meditating on it day and night, it will change you and empower you. Ask God, "What passage do you have for me? What are you speaking to me?" As a practical assignment, take a notecard and write down one Scripture that the Lord has spoken to you recently. Place it somewhere you will see often, on your desk, the dashboard of your car, etc. and meditate on it throughout the day. Slowly say it, pray it, allowing the words to transform your heart and your mind.

Date: _____

Religious Deliverance

"One of the side effects of losing intimacy with God is that at some point we stop doing ministry from intimacy, and we begin doing it out of memory."
—Bill Johnson

I want to continue in this devotional where I left off in the last one. As I continued to memorize God's Word day after day, I began to devour the Scriptures, writing on notecards passages and phrases that stirred my heart. I added to the list daily new passages and recited the ones I had done previously. After years of memorization, my rhythm of Scripture meditation lasted upwards of one hour a day.

As this continued, my stature of wisdom and knowledge began to grow rapidly. I started getting opportunities to preach and teach the Word. As I did, I found myself having the Word flow off my tongue, being able to preach without notes. Immediately people took notice, and for the years to follow, people began to comment time and time again on the fabulous memory and wisdom that God had given me in his Word.

This habit became an intense lifestyle, and for literally 1,460 days straight, I meditated on and memorized the Word of God. However, in April 2022, something strange happened. As I was doing my daily memorization, I heard a small whisper say, "Stop." My first inclination was to rebuke Satan, thinking he was scheming to get me to stop meditating on God's Word. However, as days passed, the voice continued, and I quickly realized this wasn't Satan; it was God. Let me reiterate that the habit of memorizing Scripture had become a part of who I was. It wasn't a willy-nilly routine or hobby; it was a dedicated process that I had honed with great discipline to know God and be prepared to give an account at any moment for the hope that I had in Christ. In fact, by this time, I had thousands of verses memorized with hundreds of notecards strategically organized for particular days.

These notecards had become so precious to me that when I thought through scenarios in which my physical possession would be lost, such as in a fire, I would think, "The one thing I would want to save in a situation like this would be my Bible notecards." So, when God said, "Stop memorizing Scripture," I responded, "No way." I continued for two months, day after day, memorizing

Scripture, all the time knowing that God was asking me to stop.

Two months later, I was leading a school of ministry, teaching and preaching the Word of God daily. Throughout the week, I realized God continued to beckon me to lay down my memorization of Scripture. Though I continued to resist his voice, he continued to pursue me. Halfway into the school, a friend of mine began to teach a small message on humility. As he was sharing, something within me was provoked. I remember thinking, "The portion of Jesus's heart that he has touched and discovered I know nothing about." Neither jealousy nor envy arose; rather, my heart began to groan for increased intimacy, wanting to touch what he had taken hold of.

The week continued, as the last Saturday of our school came. I suddenly found myself deeply convicted once again. That morning there was a visitor at our school; he was an acquaintance who knew nothing about me. While wrestling with this inward tension, he approached me with great seriousness and asked a simple but profound question that cut me to the heart, "Would you give up wisdom of God and knowledge about God for intimacy with God?" He then turned around and walked away. The question left me dumbfounded and in shock. In the Spirit, my jaw dropped, and I knew what I had done. I had so radically pursued wisdom and knowledge, thinking they were the essence of intimacy, that I had lost what Christ desired most with me.

Wisdom of God and knowledge about God are pathways to intimacy in his presence but can never substitute for the substance of intimacy itself. I had forgone intimacy, thinking that the stimulation of wisdom and knowledge would satisfy what my soul desired. I continued wrestling all day with this question, debating and dialoguing with God about it.

Later that evening, the conviction intensified to the point where God was pleading with me to share with another what he was inviting me into. As I stood in the back corner of the room, a young student approached me. Immediately I knew I was to share with him my rebellion against God's voice and his invitation to me to stop memorizing Scripture.

Immediately when I told him, two friends of mine across the room yelled out to me, asking me to come to sit with them. As soon as I sat down, they asked me how I memorized so much Scripture and if I could equip them in my process. I knew God was asking me once again to voice outwardly his invitation toward me inwardly. This time as soon as I did, my heart broke. They began to pray, and I began to weep. What happened next I had never experienced in my life. As I wept, my body went numb, and I began to shake. There was no power left in me to resist God's will. This lasted for five minutes until, eventually, a spirit that had attached to me left.

I sat there in shock, as what I was experiencing wasn't peace and joy; it was loneliness and sorrow. Next, God asked me, "Would you let go of your notecards and give them to your friend?" My heart sunk even deeper. These were my prized possessions. The labor of my love toward God. I had no choice. Reaching down, I grabbed four years' worth of intense memorization and handed my cards over to my friend. Though this sounds like a small act of obedience, for me, it was a dramatic moment of faith.

As I left the building late that evening, I knew immediately something had changed. The next day, the feeling of loneliness intensified, and the best way that I can describe my emotional state of the previous evening was as if I had lost a friend. At this moment, I immediately knew that I needed to begin processing with the Lord what was occurring within me. As I did, I realized that all that I had "let go of" was simply ink and paper. At this point, I knew two things: Whatever I felt I had lost the day before, I had made a deep friendship with. And secondly, whatever I had made friends with that I thought was Jesus, wasn't.

You may wonder, "I thought you wrote in the previous blog how powerful and important memorizing Scripture is. Are you now changing your mind?" No I am not. But I have learned in this journey with Jesus that obedience to his voice is paramount in my pursuit of his presence. When I began memorizing Scripture, it was in response to his voice. It was birthed from obedience. But it eventually became religion. I relied more on the memorization of written words than I did on God's presence.

This is the essence of the religious spirit. And it looks to plague us all. The religious spirit looks good, sounds good, and oftentimes even feels good. But, it is demonically inspired and masquerades as an angel of light. It will empower you to be zealous for God without God, accomplish things for God without God, and ultimately make friendship with something that seems like God but is not God.

Today, God is inviting you to let go of your friendship of feasting from the table of religious demons and to come into intimacy with the presence of God.

It's going to take courage to trust and a willingness to receive God's correction. If you will receive his correction and let go in courage, he will come and fill you with his glory.

> "Does the Lord delight in burnt offerings and sacrifices as much as in obeying the Lord? To obey is better than sacrifice, and to heed is better than the fat of rams. For rebellion is like the sin of divination, and arrogance like the evil of idolatry. Because you have rejected the word of the Lord, he has rejected you as king."
> —1 Samuel 15:22-23 (NIV)

Have I made friendship with religion?

Friendships affect us. Shape us. And make us. They are more precious than rubies and sought out after more than gold. But friendships also have the ability to kill us. Enslave us. And manipulate us. It is possible to love religion about God instead of truly loving God. If you know this is you, today ask God, "What do you want me to let go of, and what do you want me to take hold of?"

Date:

Power of Persistent Prayer

"Prevailing prayer is that which secures an answer. Saying prayers is not offering prevailing prayer. The prevalence of prayer does not depend so much on quantity as on quality." —Charles Finney

Have you ever wondered, "What is the point of prayer? Does it matter? Is God listening?" My guess is that many Christians sincerely ask these types of questions. While we all grow up learning the importance of prayer, it is not until you see the fruit of prayer that the revelation of its power and the value of your participation in it begins to personally affect your life.

It was in 2018 that I really began to discover the power of prayer. As I did, I began to notice the zeal Jesus had for it. In fact, he was so passionate about prayer that the one thing his disciples asked him to teach them how to do was pray. (Lk. 11:1.) They realized that the life and ministry of Jesus flowed from his interactive relationship (aka prayer) with his Father. Therefore, if they were going to follow in his footsteps, doing the things he was doing, they, too, would have to learn how to pray.

Not only so, but Jesus also repeatedly taught parables that explained the posture they were to take in prayer. In Luke 11 and 18, he lays out two stories, teaching his disciples the boldness and confidence they could have in prayerful conversation with God. While we often think prayer only occurs as we bow our heads, close our eyes, and timidly ask God if he would consider listening to us, Jesus taught something much different. In these two parables, he exhorts his disciples into shameless audacity and persistence in their prayer life. (Read Lk. 11:5-10, 18:1-8.)

In 2018, these Scriptures, along with many more, began to give me faith to believe in the power of persistent and bold prayer. As I began to participate in this type of prayer, I constantly heard the Lord remind me, "The only prayers that hold power are the ones that are in agreement with my heart. If you are going to pray in power, you need to hear my voice. If you're going to pray 'in the name of Jesus' you first have to discover what is in the heart of Jesus." As I meditated on this word, I realized prayer wasn't just about me speaking to God; it was about me communing with him.

In this place of communion, I discovered that God didn't only want me to speak to him; in fact, he first wanted to speak to me. Where I used to pray from my wisdom of what seemed good for God to do for others, I began to hear God's wisdom of what he wanted to do for others. Suddenly, rather than asking God to do something, I listened to what he wanted to do. Suddenly, I didn't wish for God to do something; I was simply adding my amen to what he was doing and confidently participating by faith in prayer with his heart. (1 Jn. 5:14-15.)

As I continued to grow in this, I started to learn the power of crafting prayers that I could pray continually. I began to speak less in prayer and listen more. As I did, I got caught up in the throne room of intercession and began hearing what Jesus was praying. (See Heb. 7:25.) I began to write down what I heard, crafting prayers that were in alignment with the intercession of Jesus. Without fail, I always heard a verse in the Bible that articulated the theme of Jesus's heart. It hit me, I am called to pray without ceasing. What if I redirected the distracting device called the iPhone to remind me to pray. Suddenly, I began to set dozens of alarms a day that shocked my heart into prayer. These prayer alarms would be directly set at the time that correlated with the Bible passage the Lord laid on my heart.

Suddenly, my prayer life amped up. Rather than praying once a day, I began to pray with intense persistence throughout the day. The crafted prayers piled up as, moment by moment, I began to add my amen to the prayer in the heart of Jesus.

While I have seen dozens of provisions to these types of persistent prayers, I want to share a testimony of one. In the fall of 2018, my friend Matthew was praying. As he was, he got a very specific word for my sister and brother-in-law, who at the time lived in Fresno, California. In private, he shared with me his word saying, "I believe God is saying that Jonathan and Whitney are to move back to Hillsboro, KS (the town I live in) by 2020 before having their first child." To give context, at the time, my sister had zero interest in ever returning to Hillsboro. They were not pregnant, and as far as we knew, they weren't planning to be anytime soon.

However, the word landed in my heart. As I prayed, the Lord placed the passage 2 Corinthians 1:20 in my heart. Right away, I set my alarm for 1:20pm every day, and invited my parents to persistently join me in prayer. We prayed daily for a year and a half. Suddenly, a month before 2020, Whitney and Jonathan were moving to Hillsboro a month after having their first child!

Could have or would have God orchestrated this event without our participation in persistent prayer? Maybe. I don't know. All I know is that God LOVES his sons and daughters to participate with him in prayer. He loves us being caught up with his heart in the story that he is playing out. He loves us hearing his voice and adding our amen with confidence in prayer to what he is orchestrating. I could share dozens of more stories just like this one where what we were praying came to fruition simply by listening intently, carefully crafting prayers, and praying persistently.

This persistence in prayer for my sister didn't just produce a specific outcome; it changed a person. Me. My faith skyrocketed. My understanding of authority was increased. And my persistence to pray was propelled. I love this about prayer. It changes us inwardly as much as it produces outcomes outwardly.

Just like he invited me, Jesus is inviting you to get caught up into the throne room of intercession and begin to listen and boldly pray. You don't need super emotional moments, corporate prayer meetings, or specific times in order to have power and effectiveness in your prayer life. You can simply craft a prayer, set an alarm, and pray faithfully. As you do, watch; God will respond!

*"Until now you have not asked for anything in my name.
Ask and you will receive, and your joy will be complete."*
—John 16:24 (NIV)

What has God promised and what is he exhorting me to pray?

God longs for you to know his heart, pray his will, and experience his provision. One tool you can use in partnership with the Lord is a crafted prayer. You start by recognizing the desire within your heart that has been given to you by God. As you identify this unmet desire, listen to what the Lord is saying. Ask him for specific phrases and Scriptures. As you compile what he speaks, begin writing a prayer. If helpful, answer the following questions and let them be a guide to what you craft.

1) What promise have you sensed God prophesy over your life, or where are you asking the Lord for a breakthrough?

2) What verse or passage of Scripture can you pray regarding this promise or breakthrough?

3) Spend a few minutes writing a crafted prayer asking the Father to bring to fruition what he has promised.

Date: _____

Feasting at the Table of Obedience

"Obedience is not measured by our ability to obey laws and principles, obedience is measured by our response to God's voice." —Bill Johnson

What does God delight in the most? Have you ever pondered this question? If not, I encourage you to. Because what we believe he delights in if we want to please him, will become the pursuit of our life. If we do not interpret his longing rightly, we will live a life striving to give to God what he never wanted and, ultimately, striving for what is impossible to do.

Unfortunately, many live this way. Many do not rightly perceive the heart of God. It is one of Satan's primary strategies to distort our perspective of what God delights in. If he can, either we will reject God because we do not want to give him what we think he wants. Or, we will become self-righteous in our pursuit, trying to get God to delight in us, in our doing, rather than giving him what he wants by simply just being.

When we discover that God delights in our obedience to his voice, not our duty to his commands, we will be free to live in right relationship with him. In fact, not only will we be in right relationship, we will flourish in joy in our walk alongside him. Obeying his voice is not burdensome; on the contrary, it is the pathway to be in his presence where the fullness of joy and pleasures forevermore reside.

For me, this discovery came one day as I was provoked by a brother in Christ who was passionately preaching about the power of fasting. As he did, I began to think, "I need to do that!" I didn't feel condemned by his words, but I did feel inspired. I thought, "Wow, if this is the process toward intimacy with God, then count me in; I will start tomorrow." And I did. I woke up and said, "Today, I am going to start fasting." Not two seconds passed when I heard God speak to me, saying, "I didn't ask you to fast, Jesse. The pathway to my presence isn't fasting. It is obedience. If you fast, you won't be obeying me." I said back, "Well, what about Brandon? He preached yesterday on the power of fasting and how he was encountering you in unprecedented ways?" God responded, "Brandon's fasting is obedience to my voice. Yours isn't. He isn't encountering me because he is fasting; he is encountering me because he is obeying me."

I dialogued back and forth with God, honestly feeling a little confused and even more so disbelieving of what I was hearing. I firmly said to God, "But I want to fast for you!" God gently said back, "What if I don't delight in your fasting? What if you are wanting to do something for me that I don't want?" "How can you not want me to fast?" I said back. God responded, "Because I want you to obey my voice by faith, not strive to attain my pleasure out of your effort." Wow, I thought, I guess I am not fasting. Immediately I heard the Lord say, "That's right, you're not. I want you to feast. For Brandon, fasting is his obedience. For you, feasting is."

I continued to wrestle with God. The two acts of obedience felt very different. To be honest, it was confusing and didn't seem right. Throughout the next days, as I feasted with God, not worrying about what I ate, God showed me he came to fulfill the written requirement of the law and to enact a new law, one under the umbrella of freedom, not obligation. One where I listened, heard, and obeyed his voice. He said to me, "Stop mimicking other's behavior and thinking it is obedience to my leadership. Start listening to my voice, receiving what I speak, and obeying what I ask you to do. This is the pathway to my presence and the blueprint toward abiding in and being satisfied by my love."

Jesus came so you could live under the law of the Spirit that brings life and empowers freedom. The law of the Spirit is not a license to sin, and if you live in it, you don't have to worry about misusing it. The law of the Spirit is more than a moral behavior code. It is the license you hold to validate that you have access to the presence of God. In his presence, sin is non-existent. In his presence is the power to change you to become like him. Therefore, when you surrender your life to the law of the Spirit, the fruit produced from your life will, by nature, be righteousness, holiness, and purity. You won't have to try to be better for him; you will naturally be changed by him.

I learned that the law of the Spirit is not a black-and-white code of wrong and right. It isn't a checklist you need to mark off so that you can earn a grade or good standing with your teacher. The law of the Spirit cannot be measured by behavior or compared to another's lifestyle. The law of the Spirit positions you to be in the presence of God, hear the voice of God, and have the substance that gives you the power to obey God.

Today listen to what he says, feast on his voice, and you will be empowered to do what he asks. God's delight is not in your religious duty or your perfection to keep a written list of commands. His delight is in being with you. Talking with you. Walking with you. And seeing you obey what he asks. His way is the best way. He wants your obedience because he wants you to prosper. He delights in you doing what he says because he delights in you living a successful life full of joy and purpose.

> *"In sacrifice and offering you have not delighted, but you have given me an open ear. Burnt offering and sin offering you have not required. Then I said, "Behold, I have come; in the scroll of the book it is written of me: I delight to do your will, O my God; your law is within my heart."*
> —Psalm 40:6-8 (NIV)

What is my obedience to God today?

While we can be inspired by how others live their lives with Christ, having a personal and intimate relationship with Christ is crucial for living in obedience to him rather than replication of another. Ask the Lord, "How do you want me to walk in obedience with you in this season? Is there anything that I am currently doing out of replication of another rather than obedience to your voice?"

Date:

The Journey Continues
Walk vulnerably. Share boldly. Live fearlessly.

So, how about you? What is your journey? How has God encountered your heart? How has he changed your life? Your story matters, a lot! Embrace your story with joy. The glorious parts, of course. But also the painful ones. It takes vulnerability to embrace your story. It takes boldness, and it takes courage to speak it. It takes standing on the face of fear to continue living it out. But it is worth it. You were created for it. Ultimately your story is not a witness of yourself; it is a declaration of the nature and character of God. It is attractive. God wants you to share. And many that you do not know are waiting to hear.

To be honest, this book could be endless. Each of our journeys with God includes thousands and thousands of encounters and moments of breakthroughs. Mountain top moments of joy along with valleys of despair. Though I am writing this book of my own journey, the fact is each of us was created by a God who is pursuing us relentlessly. He is not content with our mediocrity or slavery to Satan's schemes. He wants us free and flourishing in his love.

This life is a journey. The pinnacle point our heart longs to reach will never be attained in this earthly life. We were created to live in the fullness of God's glory and presence. That pinnacle will be reached one day when we see Jesus face to face and, in a moment, become the fullness of what God intended us to be. (1 Jn. 3:2.) Until that time, we each are embracing a path. I encourage you to embrace the narrow path. Embrace the journey of discomfort and death to self. Embrace the cross. Though it may be painful at times, the path is lavished with God's presence. It is lavished with God's tender lovingkindness. It is filled with his power. It was paved for you.

Walk it. You will have to learn to be weak, dependent, and trustworthy, or else you will revert to the wide road. But if you stay steadfast in the narrow lane, the life you will experience is beyond your current comprehension. I promise you; God has thousands of encounters with his glory prepared for you on that road. He has dreams and passions you long to live out. He has friends and family you do not yet know waiting for you on that path.

Today, stand up and step in. The journey you have been on in the past is powerful and the one God has planned for you in the future is even more. God has paved the path to his presence and prepared for you more than you could ever dream, ask, or imagine. Start today by choosing to walk vulnerably. Share boldly. And live fearlessly.

> "Enter through the narrow gate . . . small is the gate and narrow the road that leads to life, and only a few find it."
> —Matthew 7:13-14 (NIV)

Who can I share my journey with?

Today, spend a few minutes answering these questions and inviting someone into your journey with Jesus.

1. Ask God, "How have you encountered my life?" Sit and listen. Then begin writing the stories of your encounters with God.

2. Who do you want me to share with today? What story do you want them to hear?

*3. Text or call. Set up a meeting. And courageously share your story.
It may change a life*

Date: _____

INDEX

SECTION 1 — 19

    Seal of Fire — 21

    Coffee with God — 25

    A Royal Diadem — 29

    A Culture of Honor — 33

    The Real Thing — 37

    The Heart of the Father — 41

    His Perfect Perspective — 45

    My Fathers Presence — 49

    A Coming King — 53

    His Jealousy for Jerusalem — 57

SECTION 2 — 63

    Baptism of Love — 65

    Hope — 69

    Feasting in the Midst of Your Foes — 73

    Prophetic Sons and Daughters Arise — 77

    Betrayal — 83

    His Heart's Desire — 87

    Fear of Bad News — 91

    Surrender — 95

    Carrying His Yoke — 99

    The Way of the Wilderness — 103

SECTION 3 — 109

- Lovesick Longing — 111
- A Doorway into Intimacy — 115
- Breaking the Power of Porn — 119
- Maturing into a Child — 123
- The Beauty of Mess — 127
- Mediocrity in Marriage — 131
- Delight and Desire — 135
- An Umbrella of Love — 139
- The Destiny of a Servant — 143
- Consecrated to the King — 147

SECTION 4 — 151

- The Salvation of our Soul — 153
- A New Name — 157
- Nothing Wasted — 161
- Son of Inheritance — 165
- Discovering the Will of God — 169
- Manna to my Soul — 173
- Religious Deliverance — 177
- Power of Persistent Prayer — 183
- Feasting at the Table of Obedience — 189
- The Journey Continues — 193

About the Author

Born and raised in Hillsboro, KS, Jesse Allen is passionate about partnering with Jesus to raise up a generation that radically loves Jesus and longs for his return. Shortly after graduating from Tabor College in 2016, Jesse's heart began to yearn for the next generation and the nations while he and his wife Tara served in Thailand for seven months as part of a Mennonite Brethren missions program known as TREK.

After serving alongside the local church planters in Thailand, Jesse and Tara moved back to Hillsboro where they now live with their two daughters, Kinsley and Harper. In 2021, Jesse earned a Master's of Science in Ministry, Entrepreneurship, and Innovation from Tabor College. Along with his passion for continued learning, Jesse has a deep passion for teaching the Word of God. He is the author of Loving the Lord's Anointed as well as the co-author of The Supremacy of Christ. He also partners with a Wichita-based ministry called Disciple Nations, through which he serves and equips the body of Christ to know their identity in Jesus and walk out their destiny in the kingdom of God.

Currently Jesse helps lead a non-profit ministry called Kingdom Equip. Through a variety of initiatives, such as running a house of prayer, a yearly discipleship training school, and a regular equipping service for the body of Christ, Kingdom Equip exists to raise up a generation to love Jesus and long for his return. Jesse desires that his writings can help ignite this initiative and place a burning love for Jesus into the heart of those who read his work. Visit Kingdom Equip at https://www.kingdomequip.school

Made in the USA
Monee, IL
27 April 2023

32473512R00111